Death and Birth of the Parish

Death and Birth

of the Parish

MARTIN E. MARTY, EDITOR AND AUTHOR
with
PAUL R. BIEGNER, ROY BLUMHORST
and
KENNETH R. YOUNG

CONCORDIA
Saint Louis

Concordia Publishing House, St. Louis, Missouri
Concordia Publishing House Ltd., London, W. C. 1
© 1964 Concordia Publishing House

Library of Congress Catalog Card No. 64-23370

Manufactured in the United States of America

Preface

Some years ago I read a book review which dealt with the subject of the local congregation in the modern world. The reviewer argued that "it is possible to see the modern parish as an entity to be created rather than a survival to be preserved." Ever since, it has seemed to me that discussion of local churches should be carried on not with a view as to what can be saved from the past but rather as to what would God work in the present and the future.

In 1964 an international organization of Lutheran laymen announced that they intended to discuss the parish. Pastor Roland H. A. Seboldt, upon hearing of this intention, encouraged me to edit a book which would serve their purposes as well as those of any Christians who are concerned with the divine commands and promises as they affect local situations. As book editor of Concordia Publishing House he proposed the names of three pastors who might write about the kinds of situations in which most parishes work today. We met to outline the book and agreed at once that what laymen and serious pastors do not need is "one more program." They receive much good advice as to how to work with existing parishes. Less often do they ask the basic questions of "the thing" itself.

Those who are looking (may I use a well-worn metaphor?) for a band-aid to put on a cancer will find little here to interest them. We have a surgical interest, believing that radical surgery can be a step toward healing. Those who are looking for the One Big Answer will also be disappointed. None of us believes that in our complex modern world anyone can come up with a magic secret which will make the local congregation meaningful and effective. We are united in our belief that patient attention to detail: the detail of the Scripture, Christian history, our culture, and modern modes of ministry, will be more rewarding.

Many professional theologians and social analysts have written about the parish; it is a truism that little of this theological talk or social language "trickles down" to practical parish life. It is our hope that ministers who are informed by the professional inquiries but who daily live with practical parish life can serve to bridge or to translate from one community of concern to another. We hope that this book will be read, discussed, "torn apart," and put together again by the people who make up local parishes. Our ideas, our proposals — to borrow the theme of the book — also have to "die" * in order to live.

One minor technical point is in order. For many centuries the word "parish" carried with it a territorial meaning: all the people within a certain area were the responsibility of one pastoral charge. In the modern world this territorialism has broken down. Perhaps one should always speak of "local congregation" or "local church," terms which are in our usage synonymous with "parish." We are using that word in this modern dictionary sense: "a local ecclesiastical society or organization, usually not bounded by territorial limits, but composed of those persons who

---

* In choosing our title we acknowledge the influence of Walter Kloetzli's *City Church — Death or Renewal* (Philadelphia: Muhlenberg, 1961). The four authors of the book deliberated as to whether the title should imply "rebirth" or "birth." For a number of reasons we chose the more radical term. Numbers of studies have spoken of renewal or rebirth as if all that is needed in the forms of church life is a minor readjustment or streamlining. We believe that more risk is involved. We are not sure whether minor adaptations will serve. "Birth" implies God's new creation of new forms. Of course the term must be taken as an illustration of the process of change and is not meant literally. Where the divine Word is present, "death" in the usual sense of the term cannot be. But just as that Word kills off all that is old in the sinner, so it may kill — in order to vivify — all that is old in the fellowship of sinners.

choose to unite under the charge of a particular clergyman or minister." Of course we immediately move beyond that language of choosing to speak of how God the Holy Spirit "chooses" his church through the Good News of Jesus Christ.

I have found editor Seboldt and the three contributing pastors to be extremely congenial company. Having edited a number of books before this one, I have a background out of which to note one remarkable feature of these contributors' work: they were all punctual in submitting their manuscripts. Having observed two of them in their parish routines, I can witness that their work was done in hours rescued from the end or the start of the day, and I am grateful to them for the sacrifices they have made. Since many of their analyses and proposals may look controversial, I must also thank them for venturing to respond to the request to write. May the church people who read and employ this book receive it in the spirit of the authors. We know that the church, finally, does not live by our analyses and proposals but by the promises of God.   M. E. M.

Contents

Death and Birth of the Parish

Martin E. Marty

Death and Birth of the Parish

Around the Christian world there are hundreds of thousands of local gatherings of people. These are called, variously, congregations or local churches or parishes. Since this form of Christian gathering is so widespread and visible, it is the form that most regularly comes under study and criticism. Not all Christians can observe in detail what is going on in seminaries and colleges, denominational offices and publishing houses. But right before their eyes is a congregation made up of people they know, doing things in which they can participate. Inevitably the local congregation becomes the subject of much praise and much criticism by laymen who have not had to do too much general thinking about the nature of the whole Christian church in the world.

In a revolutionary time like our own it is only natural that study of the parish should be intensified. Today we take nothing for granted that we have inherited. Our most beloved traditional forms seem to fail us. We are unsure of our footing — the ground seems to move beneath us — and we are unsure of where to look because the skies are clouded. In such a time a traditional form like the parish may easily be rejected because it does not change enough to help us meet the real problems of our lives. Thus many laymen reject the parish without thinking too much about it.

Thoughtful Observers Are Divided

The thoughtless rejection of the local church by unthinking people is not our first concern in this book. We are going to focus our attention on the notice being given the parish by thoughtful students of the forms of Christian life. Some of these students are missionaries and some are theologians, some are historians and social scientists, and others are educators or liturgists. Today as never before the parish is being studied by professional observers of institutions. What they find is most disturbing.

A typical meeting of these students or critics of the churches will soon fall into one of two or three patterns. At the base of each pattern, one can predict, there will be a nearly unanimous agreement by all present that the parish as we have inherited it is not doing the task and cannot do the task to which Christ has committed His church in the world. In other words the parish is sick — deathly sick. The participants in the meeting will gather around their subject, the parish, just as surgeons in a medical school gather around a patient on the operating table. These participants will then discuss what to do about the sick patient, the local congregation. Some will suggest a prescription. Give it a few pills and pep it up, and it will live for a while and somehow get to be "up and around." A second group will advocate surgery: Cut deep and far; do some grafting and transplanting; sew with care and heal with concern. Out of such radical surgery may come health. A third group may say, in effect: The patient is too far gone. If we devote our attention to him, we may be diverted from some that we could save. We will be busy devoting ourselves to a hopeless case and letting others become hopeless cases. Let this one alone and let us be about our real work. A fourth group is more hasty. It seems to be saying: This patient is taking up time and space which should be given to another. Administer euthanasia; kill him off. Get him out of the way so that we can be about our business.

You might say, "Someone is missing from the deliberations of these surgeons." If so, you may be correct. Many different kinds of "someones" do not come to such consultations. Who is missing?

4

Some are not welcome. Those who see no sickness in the patient and announce that they refuse to see any will not be welcome. They appear too blind or too prejudiced to deserve attention. Still less welcome are those who know there is a sickness but believe it can be talked away without prescription or surgery. These are the "positive thinkers" who say "peace" when there is no peace; "grace" where there is only sin; "health" where there is disease. Such people when they look at the consultation of surgeons announce to the world: There is nothing at all wrong with the patient. The professional fee splitters have gathered to swoop in like vultures. They are morbid. They do not look for health and do not recognize it when it comes. They do not want the patient to look healthy, and by their attitudes and words they only succeed in convincing the patient and all of us that there is disease.

Between these two groups of people — the students or critics of the parish on the one hand and the defenders of the parish as it is on the other hand — are the mass of Christian people. They are understandably bewildered when they hear of a debate of the kind we have just described. For one thing, many of them are unprepared. They did not know that any such debate or conversation was going on. They were preoccupied with matters of world and church, and these particular matters were never called to their attention. They may have had hunches that all things around them, including the forms of church life, were being subjected to radical change. But the details that would confirm these hunches escaped them or were kept from their notice. For another thing, to many Christians life in their local parish is so rich and so meaningful that they cannot understand why parishes are so much the object of study and the subjects of so much criticism. The missionaries and theologians, educators and moralists seem to look at congregations "from the outside," they reason. But if they would "come on in" and participate they would find more meaning and fulfillment in parish life.

5

When Thoughtful Pastors Observe Parishes

The major portions of this book are written by men who are pastors to Christian people. None of these pastors have, to our knowledge, been previously identified either with the radical critics or passionate defenders of the parish. They speak to and for the kind of faithful Christians who have the hunches about change around them, the hope for Christian change through themselves, and the willingness to look at change as a possibility for themselves. Not often do we have the opportunity to "eavesdrop," as it were, on busy pastors. Ministers of local churches are usually defensive if their churches are subjected to criticism or defeatist if their churches do not subject themselves to criticism.

Our writers are young but already experienced ministers in typical situations of the inner city, the suburb, or the small town and the country. They are men of above average theological and intellectual interest, but men who are ordinarily putting their talents to work in a ministry of Word and Sacrament in routine parish situations. Why are they writing? The answer is simple — they were asked to. We "stopped them in their tracks" and asked them to look not at *their* parishes (this would be poor taste in public print) but at *the* parish as it is seen in the light of their work.

Where do the authors of this book fit in the cast of characters we have described above? They are not at all on the side of the uncritical defenders or the positive thinkers. As professional clergy, they are not given the luxury of "sitting out the debate." That takes care of clusters two and three, and leaves us only with the first group — the surgeons. Do they offer simple prescriptions or seek radical surgery; do they want to let the patient die or do they want to kill him off? If we want to press our picture to the limits, we could say they urge radical surgery. But the title of this book suggests that they go further than this. They talk about "death," and they talk about "birth." They talk about

6

forms that have to die and about forms that will replace them —
about a spirit of disease and death that has to be supplanted by
a spirit of health and life and newness. This, it seems to me, is
the distinctive element in their talking about the parish.

The kind of language they use is unfamiliar to many of us.
Or so we think, until we reflect for a while and find that we are
applying it to Christian individuals all the time. When a Christian speaks about his personal life and health, he is trained to
talk in radical terms. He has a "sickness unto death" and lives in
the despair of separation from God. How does he come to health
and life? Is he helped by a prescription, a pill which makes the
temperature go away? Is he helped if he is abandoned to death
or "killed off" — and that killing off is the end of the story? Is he
helped, from the other side, by those who tell him that nothing
is wrong and that he will be all right, if only he thinks he is all
right and if only he does not listen to those who tell him something is wrong? Is he helped if he is unmindful of his health
and spiritual life? The answer to all these questions, as any
spiritual director will affirm, is an emphatic no.

Whoever has read his Bible and observed the ministry of
Jesus' life will know why the answer has to be no. They have
heard Jesus say, "Those who are well have no need of a physician,
but those who are sick; I came not to call the righteous, but
sinners" (Mark 2:17). Whoever has read his Bible and observed
the ministry of Jesus' death will also know why the answer has
to be no. They have heard Paul say of it, "We were buried therefore with Him by baptism into death, so that as Christ was raised
from the dead by the glory of the Father, we too might walk in
newness of life" (Rom. 6:3). The difficult jump for most people
to make is to take these references to the individual sick man or
sinner or the isolated Christian walking in newness of life and
apply them to a sick and sinful church or a church walking in
newness of life.

7

Perhaps we have forgotten the language of Paul with its accent on "bearing one another's burdens." Perhaps we have so thoughtlessly adopted the language of individualism that we have forgotten the language of the church: "As one man's trespass led to condemnation for all men, so one man's act of righteousness leads to acquittal and life for all men" (Rom. 5:18). Those who are in Christ have a common destiny — they are to be raised to new life with their Head, who has been raised. "Now you are the body of Christ and individually members of it." (1 Cor. 12:27)

Pastors use this language whenever they preach. Sin is a personal and individual matter, *and* it is a communal and social matter. The pastor would not be able to preach, he could only hear private confession, if he were not able to deal with the disease, sin, and death of the congregation. He can generalize and he can preach Law, because he knows of the common plight of the whole congregation, and he can preach the Good News of the new life, because he knows of God's act of reconciliation involving not isolated individuals but the whole gathering. Just as the pastor does to his own flock, the pastors in this book and the observers for whom they speak apply the terms of death and new birth to the situation of the parish anywhere in the Christian world.

The Parishes Look Healthy

The time has come for a more detailed and careful analysis of the issues involved in the matter of death and new birth in the parish. We can do this best by listening first to those who suggest that there is no disease, no failure that should cause us to look at congregational life so carefully. Their arguments are full of practical wisdom and vitality. Listen to them. For one thing, there are today more parishes in the world and more people in them than ever before. The number of congregations is growing, and the total number of Christians is growing. Obviously great

8

numbers of people invest a great amount of hope in them. Why criticize an institution which is so successful at spreading itself, enlarging itself?

Second, these local congregations express a great deal of variety. There are large ones and small ones, rich ones and poor ones, well located and poorly located ones. Some build great churches, and others worship in rented halls and homes. Some have a good name in their communities, and others are despised. Some have long traditions, and others have the freshness of youth. In such a range of variety, cannot one say that parishes adapt well to the many changes and many kinds of life a revolutionary time gives us? One could go on. Without doubt many of these congregations are staffed with men and women who are better craftsmen than their predecessors, and they have better tools for spreading the healing message. Only a romantic can overlook the faults of parishes in the past, and yet despite these faults the church survived. Whoever has read Luther's description of the German congregations in his introduction to his Small Catechism or whoever has read of the status of parishes in England when John Wesley began his work knows of ignorance and superstition and even corruption in those times. Yet the raw material for reformation and renewal among people was in those parishes. It is important not to compare today's parish with a supposedly perfect model in a presumed set of "good old days" in the past. Today's people and their pastors can be and often are better trained students of the Bible and more informed participants in church life than their forefathers were. Should this not count for something?

In reckoning with reasons why the parishes should perhaps not be subjected to scrutiny, the most important factor is the widespread regard in which they are held. What should one say of the faithfulness with which Christian people support their local congregations? Many of them attend divine services regularly;

9

some of them make real financial sacrifices each week; who can count the millions of man-hours and woman-hours devoted each week to selfless service of God through local parishes? In fact there is so much membership, attendance, support, sacrifice, and activity today that for many people the word "church" means "my local congregation" and almost all the physical and spiritual energies devoted to the church are devoted to or through the local congregation. Is not that a mark of the adaptability and success of the parish?

The Critics Are Not Satisfied

None of these factors count for much to the critics of the parish. If we look at who some of these are, we shall be able to determine much about the two sides in the Cold War of interpretation which afflicts (but which may ultimately benefit) the Christian church today. Almost everyone who studies the context or the social setting of the church in the world today comes to one set of conclusions. Who are these students; what are their vocations and their presuppositions?

We cannot any longer hide the word: many of them are sociologists. Sociology is a perfectly respectable discipline in the universities. Where there is not good professional sociology there is good or bad amateur sociology going on at all times. The same minister who uses the word "sociologist" as if it referred to some creepy, crawly thing is himself in a way a sociologist to the extent that he knows where his people live, what they do for a living, how regular they are at church, what are their hobbies and hopes. Whenever he counts noses, tabulates returns, grows suspicious of motives, or tries to summarize elements of social life, he is an amateur sociologist. Why is this kind of minister so filled with sneers when he looks at the work of the professional social scientist when that work is directed to the church?

There are good and bad reasons for his mistrust. The good

reasons can be summarized under two headings. For one thing, not everything in the life of the church can be subjected easily to the observation of social scientists. There is an essential hiddenness to much Christian response, and because of this many important elements of the Christian life will escape the sociologists' notice. For another, no one works without some presuppositions, and the critic of sociology knows that sociologists have their own working assumptions, assumptions which may color and prejudice what they turn up.

For example, one of the sociological studies of marriage on my shelves informs me that the sociologists in question did not take the couples' religion into account in a study "because sociologists have traditionally viewed church membership as a conventional matter unlikely to signify much about the persons involved." [1] Further down the same shelf are dozens of books by sociologists who view church membership as a factor which tells a great deal about persons. As another example: Some sociologists work or used to work on lines of interpretation which we might associate with Karl Marx (which is not the same thing as saying they were or are communists!). By this I mean to say only that they suggest that if one knows all about a person's economic position and political life one can predict a great deal about his religion.

Yet more sociologists work on an opposing line of interpretation, associated loosely with the name of Max Weber. This line suggests that if one knows a great deal about one's basic religious faith and commitments, he can begin to predict what economic and political attitudes and forms his life will take. Sociology of religion is itself a house divided; why, asks the mistrustful Christian, should one be bothered with these varying interpretations?

If some dismiss social science because it tells us too little about religion, others have a less worthy motive in dismissing it — it tells too much. One of the most effective critics of American religion from the viewpoint of social science is the Lutheran layman Peter Berger. Berger has noted that today the traditional assaults on the churches by Biblical critics, evolutionists, and Freudian psycho-analysts seldom seem so threatening as do the more recent "assaults" by sociologists. The loss of innocence and the shock of recognition ("We did not know we were being watched!" "He's got our number!") serve to create great defensiveness in the churches. Any church body which has permitted social scientists to have access to its members and to make intensive studies (based on polls and interviews) concerning members' attitudes to sex and marriage or concerning the real interests of youth will recognize the shock which the results and reports produce. These reports usually suggest that most of the time we live in a world of self-delusion; we do not like to have self-knowledge.

So the critics of the critics accuse social scientists (as I heard one once say) of "sticking their noses in limburger cheese and then running around complaining that the whole world smells." What they fail to notice is that, to borrow the picture, the soci-ologists regularly wipe their noses clean, but almost everywhere they dip them again they come up with limburger cheese. And when they note the exception and come up smelling of roses and balsam, their professional reputation depends on the ability with which they can convey their findings about sweet smells!

Social scientists, of course, are not infallible. Their methods need constant criticism. They work in academies and universities, settings which may color their views of religion and parishes. But they are not alone. Theologians who subject the reality of the parish to the pictures given us in the Bible regularly express dismay at what they find. Sometimes theologians are naive about social science and especially about history. They act as if "once upon a time" there were parishes that were perfectly organized to fulfill God's purposes and that only today they are failing.

12

I know of a magazine which has a standard answer when people write in and say, "Your magazine is not as good as it used to be." The editors write an answer: "You are right. And it never was." So with the parish. It never was "as good as it used to be." Which is another way of saying that each generation has to do its own task of examining itself in the light of the ideal picture given us in the command and promise of Christ. And the theologian who compares that command and promise to the reality of our parishes today does have plenty to complain about in what he sees.

Missionary Thinkers Are Often Disturbed

To my mind more important and more telling criticism than that which comes from sociologists and theologians comes from missionary thinkers and strategists. Indeed in public they are often quite amiable. They must be content to go along with "the best we now have," the existing forms of congregational life. They have to be content to pick up the financial crumbs and to work on the basis of the leftover imagination and energy of people in the parish. But when they are given the opportunity, almost all of them are more searching. Picture yourself in the situation of a man charged with bringing the message of Jesus Christ to people around the world in the name of, say, a 2.5 million-member denomination made up of perhaps 5,000 parishes. You travel and see a world of desolation and despair, a world — as you see it — in need of Christ and of bread. Then you come home and tour the denomination. You see people investing luxuriously in church parlors and cushioned pews and each year tossing a tip (say, for example, $3.00) for the whole worldwide work of the church. Would it not occur to you that every brick placed in the wall of such a parish church is a brick placed over against a world of need? What is worse, you enter these walls and find that they not only commit a congregation financially but they obscure the vision of the real world from people. That

13

is, people lose their imagination for the remote. They live in the illusion that everyone could have their standards and way of life. They lose sympathy for the people who are screened off from their view.

As an illustration I will refer to the work of a sociologist (pardon me) who took a survey of attitudes in a metropolitan area to the idea of sending food to a nation in need. Should one first look at the reality of hunger, the neighbor in need, the pangs of despair, the outstretched hand? Or does one begin by asking the question of means: where do we get the ships? Or the question of consequences: what will this do to our economy and to our political relations to other nations? (The country in question in his survey was not an enemy but a "neutral.") Whoever has read the story of the Good Samaritan or the Judgment Day parable ("Whatever you have done to the least of my brethren . . .") will know what the expected Christian answer will be. First look at human need in the Christ who is disguised in our brothers. Then find the means and relate the consequences.

But this careful sociologist turned up what so consistently comes about when such surveys are made. The humanist, nonbelieving, and agnostic elements of the community were most generous; Jews were second; Roman Catholics, third; Negro Protestants were fourth. Finally, white Protestants — and the most active white Protestants were most economically protective. First see what the problem does to our economy; see if we can spare food; see what it does to our alliances. If everything is perfectly safe and good for America, then take up the possibility of sharing! (No wonder many church people do not like social scientists!) Such surveys point up the fact that our parishes as they now exist often commit us to a kind of chumminess and "clubbiness" with our kind of people which makes us unsympathetic with others. Is not the parish that produces or is produced by such fraternization diseased and dying? Would not new birth be greatly desired?

14

The missionary, then, is joined by social workers and deaconesses and heads of benevolent agencies. They see the local parishes — with which they must work with a smile and with "chins up" — to be, too often, incarnations of prejudices along lines of race and class. Benevolent societies used to have little difficulty portraying the drama of need among orphans. They have great difficulty doing so about delinquents or Negro children on the Aid to Dependent Children rolls. Why? Because in our parishes "no one" is of "that type," and we are vehement in rejection of the way of life and the kind of people that do not keep our standards and who produce delinquents or illegitimate children. Why support an agency which works with them?

Can the Parish Be Changed to Serve?

When these questions are raised, one wonders whether the parish can ever be adapted or reborn to serve Christ's cause in a revolutionary world. Have the defenders of the parishes as they are "taken the future seriously"? One cannot help but be impressed by what Gunnar Myrdal calls "the Great Awakening," an explosive process by which 1.5 billion people who were born into societies of ancient and changeless outline have suddenly been jolted into awareness of modernity. Robert Heilbroner comments: "Nothing so grandiose — and nothing so disruptive — has ever happened in history." The change is revolutionary, not evolutionary. Comments Heilbroner: This is a *colored* revolution of black, yellow, and brown millions. "It will not be easy for a nation that systematically insults the sensibilities of the colored tenth of its population to exert a natural leadership over its course." [2] The missionary thinkers and ethical leaders who see the Christian parishes as chief locations of racial separateness and prejudice know that such parishes are immobilized in a mission to these 1.5 billion people.

From their point of view Christian mission in what used to be

15

called "the non-Christian world" has virtually ground to a halt. As mission scholar R. Pierce Beaver put it some years ago: missions now means a vast system of mutual interchurch aid and not the establishment of new beachheads where the Christian presence has not been known. Some 91% of the world's Roman Catholics (and, we presume, Protestants) are in Old and New Europe — which includes North and South America. About 9% are elsewhere. But 70% of the world's people live in that "elsewhere," and their part of the world is growing faster. Can the existing forms of Christian life, including settled, static, secure parishes, ever be mobilized to serve in such a setting? Whoever loves his Lord and the church and whoever takes the future really seriously, it would seem, should take serious and critical views of forms of church life which are failing. So the missionary thinkers begin by saying: This one thing we know. What we now have is not doing the job. Perhaps some change can be brought about which could begin to do it.

On the other side of our Cold War are those pastors and lay leaders who — let us give them full credit — are really doing whatever they can to carry on the works of love where they are. They cannot all pack off and go to Tanganyika. They cannot all give full time to the church. They cannot all live in the inner city. But they can keep their eye on "the city which has foundations whose builder and maker is God" (Heb. 11:10). Their lives often shame the lives of social scientists and theologians and missionary thinkers. They give tirelessly of their energies; they spread the Good News of God's activity; they would be embarrassed to have their work cited and applauded by the world. They are often mystified by the critics' pictures. The church is, to them, a real center of life. Here they bring up their children according to divine commands and promises. Here they see the works of love carried out. Here they see real generosity, the overcoming of division and pettiness, the concord and harmony

16

which inspires people. Here they have a place to stand to view the world. Here in their parish is a resource center from which they can go out incognito, as it were, to work the works of God in their daily life. They will listen to suggestions for improvement. They will be somehow responsive to God's judgments. But they are resentful of those who force them into a position where they have to say, "Pardon us for living." They do not like to be portrayed in a situation in which their religious disinterest would be condemned but their religious interest is too. They do not like to be told that they are "damned if they do and damned if they don't" participate in church life. They do not want a dead-ending criticism, and thus they strike back at social criticism which is not mindful of the totality of Christian life.

When Suspicion Is Present

What can be done about a Cold War which involves such well-equipped and well-meaning partisans — on both of whose sides there seems to be so much Christian witness and warrant? What are the stakes involved? We can see dilemmas all over the field as we try to answer. Suppose both sides are right. The parish as we know it may be obsolete — a problem for Christian mission and service. But the parish may be necessary for the carrying out of a certain part of Christian mission and service. Caught in such a dilemma we are insecure, and insecurity creates suspicion.

When suspicion is directed from within the parish to outside critics, it usually sounds something like this: Critics like to be critical. They make their living from criticism. They draw attention to themselves by being dramatic. (Who can sell a book full of compromise and prose and whispers?) These critics enjoy the luxury of professional pessimism: sometimes it is therapeutic to use the language of total criticism and despair. The social scientists are biased, applying methods which cannot produce Christian results. The theologians apply impossibly high standards. The

17

missionaries are impatient, looking for the Big Answer immediately and suddenly. They are all removed from the routines and quiet drama of daily life. They are awed by the principalities and powers of the world, by the way the world counts power, and they want the church to be numbered among the powers. They misread the signs of personal life and eternal hope; they confer the wrong status on Christian service in a this-worldly context. One could extend the list indefinitely, but these complaints are representative.

When suspicion is countered by suspicion, we hear charges something like this from Christians who look with criticism at the parish. The pastors, naturally, will defend the institutions which pay their groceries. They have a vested interest in the organizations which pay their salaries. They and lay leaders are concerned with the short-range view of Christian mission and service: so long as things go well in their own environment, they let the world "go to pieces." They live in a world of self-delusion. They distort statistics and intentionally misread them so that they can "keep their own show on the road." They are compromisers: they will see Christian vision dimmed by the politics of parish factionalism. They will only push people "as far as the traffic will bear." They are too much involved in the parish to be distant enough to be critical. They are romantics, dreaming of a future in which the Christian parish will again take on meaning. They are so close to the local situation that they lose perspective and are the worst judges of the effectiveness of their work. They are at the center of parish life and they naturally receive the greatest comforts and rewards of that life. They do not notice how much at the margin of most peoples' lives church membership may be or how much of a tangent to the real circles of their lives the church may have become.

Such is the language of suspicion.

The Choice Is Crucial

Suppose, for a change, we drop the language of suspicion. Many social scientists, theologians, ethical and missionary thinkers and strategists do not sound at all like those caricatured in our picture of a Cold War. They are themselves, to all appearances, faithful and humble Christian believers, regular in their own participation in the parishes which they are scrutinizing. And thousands of Christian pastors and lay leaders of our acquaintance are not at all so foolish, blind, prejudiced, and innocent of reality as our caricature of the Cold War defender of the parish seemed to be. They are self-critical, subjecting the forms of their life together to the norms of God's law and human observation. They really want to do the right thing. Cannot we advance the conversation, then, by deciding not to read the worst motives into people? Let us see what happens if we read the best and most generous motives into their activity and words and ask two important sets of questions.

What if faithful Christians chose to disregard the social thinkers and critics of the parish and they were then found to have been correct? What if, because of short-sightedness and ignorance, the church takes the wrong path and fails in its mission and service?

We cannot pretend that because we take the future seriously we can control the future. Only God can do that. We cannot manipulate mission and contrive service; only He in His freedom and grace can do that. But we can use our sense and sensibility to read the signs of the times, to be ready and open for choice in the kinds of future He chooses to give us. Suppose we know better and yet close off that future because we do not want to listen to people who may have suggestions.

What if, from the other side, the pastoral thinkers were correct all along and the church listened only to the social and missionary thinkers? What if we took a wrong turn in administering euthanasia to the forms of the parish? What if we sinned in abandoning

19

forms of Christian life which may have had much to say to our time? What if we by our actions "let the Word of God be bound" among us (for we cannot really bind it itself) so that it is not preached to the joy and edifying of Christ's holy people? What if we become so enamoured of a Grand Plan and a great design that we forget, in the mass of sociological statistics, the importance of quiet personal witness and service? What if . . . what if . . .?

Both sides, let us say, may produce people who are honest and self-critical, who subject their views to systematic study and scrutiny. Perhaps they are both looking at opposite sides of one problem and one reality and they should be brought together. Someone must take a first step at bridging the conversation in our churches between the informed people of goodwill on both sides. This book is written, as it were, from one side. None of the four authors is either a professional sociologist, academic theologian, or denominational or ecumenical missionary strategist. All four have been active in pastoral work and three still are; these are pastors who have been informed by sociologists, theologians, strategists. (We hope one day this book could be complemented by one in which sociologists, theologians, and missionary thinkers who have been informed by pastors would write of "death and birth" in the parishes!)

Does not this pastoral side prejudice the case? Since the second word of the death/birth polarity in the title of the book is "birth" with its ring of newness and hope, is not our case prejudged? Is not the suspense removed? Who will really take the future seriously if everything in that future is going to turn out all right in the end anyhow? "It won't hurt a bit" if, at the end of the operation, everything has come to a happy conclusion. To answer these legitimate questions we can only say that because we are dealing with the future, we are dealing with suspense. We may prejudge some elements of the present, but we know absolutely nothing about the future except that nothing shall befall the church in that future without the heavenly Father's knowing and caring and doing. We do not know whether there should be renewed parishes or new forms in the future. God can do without the arbitrary and accidental features of the forms our histories have given us, and still do His work. But we can point to choice in the present. Therefore, we must say, the authors here are not under the delusion that this modest study will either "kill off" or "keep alive" the parishes. They hope it will be used in the parishes where people live and think and act, where they make choices which from the human side will affect the future. The death/birth motif will help them and the authors keep the issues tense, open, and radical.

The Background of Criticism

In the brief space given me I shall try to summarize the leading positions of the social analysts of parish life. We begin by reference to what is "given" or assumed in the analyses of many of them before they undertake their criticism.

1. The world is now "rounding itself off" without reference to God or the church in most decisive areas of life: personal morality, public issues, and philosophies of life. It is doing this work of closing itself off without openness to God in the presence of widespread and strong forms of religious life, notably a nearly universal skein or strand of local congregations. They are not now effective at interrupting this rounding-off and closing-off process which is often called "secularization."

2. The most prevalent and recognized form of Christian organization is the parish or local congregation. It is therefore to be the first and most profound subject of inquiry. All the other institutions to be studied come in in secondary ways because of the immediate and personal part the parish plays in the typical Christian's life.

21

3. The current parish system is mislocated in the populations of the world. Most parishes are where fewest people are, where population growth is least dramatic. Christians in some cases get "better and better at what they have been good" and "worse and worse at what they have been bad." That is, they are more firmly located and entrenched in the dwindling white middle classes of Europe and North America while they are losing South America and failing to gain a real foothold in emerging Asia and Africa. The current parish system does not seem capable of dramatizing to Christians the seriousness of their failure or of mobilizing their imagination and energies to change.

4. Under the current system it is an accomplished fact that Christian missions have virtually ended their sense of "newness" in approach to places. There may be more missionaries in the field and more expenditures than ever before. But the percentage of Christian population has tapered to somewhere around 1% in many Asian and African nations; perhaps organizing Christian energies in some other way than in parishes would be better than what we now have.

5. The churches in the "old" West of Europe have been tried and, in the eyes of most Europeans, been found wanting. There, in what is often called the "post-Christian" world, the parishes are the centers of dead tradition, while what is new seems to come from other forms of life such as "lay academies" of study, prayer, and service. Perhaps we can learn from these forms.

6. The churches in the "new" West of North America play a more vital part in people's lives. Most Americans (somewhere over 80%) are content with traditional symbols for divine reality and affirm belief in God, the Trinity, the divinity of Christ, the authority of the Bible. They do not want to be thought of as irreligious or secularized. They participate in occasional religious revivals and in the past decade have joined churches as

22

never before. But these traditional symbols do not seem to take life in personal morality, according to most surveys; and these church memberships do not issue in a new kind of public morality. On the national scale, most personal and public decisions are made by people in such a way that one cannot see the difference in being a Christian. The parishes are the main centers of resource and motivation; if religion in America is failing, it is in the parishes that the failing is most evident. The churches are so adapted to existing cultural forms that they have difficulty getting out of their easy-chair existence to judge and redeem people. Perhaps a word from beyond the parishes will serve better than a word in the parishes.

One hears these "given" items in student gatherings, in youth conferences, at missionary meetings, in the seminaries. In Europe theologians speak of parishes as the centers of "four-wheel" Christendom; one is wheeled to church in baby buggies, nuptial limousines, and funeral hearses for three great rituals, but between these the church does not mean much. One is hatched, matched, dispatched, and the churches sanction these activities, but they have little further effect on living.

A Systematic Analysis of Parishes

The social analysts move from these "givens" to a systematic examination of the forms of death in the parish. If they are oriented toward theology, they ask questions of the faithfulness of the basic form of parish life. The Book of Acts or the Pastoral Epistles in the New Testament are often claimed as the basis for many forms of church life which are really accidental. One takes the forms of congregational activity and then clumsily backs up into the New Testament to prove that this is what God had in mind all along. In this way details of stewardship life and polity are determined — often casually. Actually very, very little of congregational life is commanded. There must be some sort of provision for preaching and participating in the Sacrament. There must be some order, some outlet for service. Almost all the rest is arbitrary. There are few prescriptions about building, organization, programs. Many historical forms are worthwhile and legitimate; many of them may be derived from Biblical commands. But one is not tampering with a holy word of God if he asks questions about ladies' aids and Boy Scouts and parish suppers and stewardship drives and voters' meetings — all of them in part accidental and practical forms of Christian expression.

The critics also are trying to purge Christians of their tendency to use the parish system of the Middle Ages as the model for today. Often people talk as if we could solve our problems if we could only go back to the parishes known then. We may learn from the medieval parish, but we cannot go back to it. Today, unlike then, the church is not officially established as part of public life; it is not supported by public funds in many countries; it does not unify community life (how can it when congregations are in competition in a locality?); it is now, as it was not then, culturally and socially possible not to be Christian. It is precisely the unified world of the Middle Ages which has broken down, and the parish adapted to that unified world is no model for today.

Nor, say the critics, will the congregation of the Reformation period serve as the model. The parishes of that time largely retained the forms of the Middle Ages. One belonged to the same church to which his prince or other ruler belonged. True, preaching was to attract people to the churches, across political lines. But such attraction was relatively rare until modern times, when people were free to join "the church of their choice" in a free society.

When one has purged himself of the belief that the churches today can and should be modeled on these three earlier forms, he is free to subject them to scrutiny in new ways. Much that

24

is accidental or abitrary is often defended as being central and vital. These accidents usually grew out of a church which had a settled and static place in the community. Today people are on the move, free to join any church or no church. Today denominationalism forces competition on congregations. Today when people join a congregation they surrender most routine religious decision to it; this is most noticeable in the use of funds. In modern Protestantism congregations defend their "autonomy" and many send on only what they choose. Most energies are devoted to the local in a day when people's consciousness is more superlocal (national, international) than it could have been in the past before modern communications developed.

From Form to Mission

After they have looked at the question of basic forms, they proceed to enlarge upon the question of missions. To the critics the parish is best adapted for a kind of game of musical chairs in evangelism. All the churches work to gain converts from the same class and batch of people in the community. Few have much desire or success when they leave the class which makes up their majority (usually the middle class) and try to work with intellectuals or workers, or especially with members of other races. Ministers often work on the assumption that their churches reach from the very rich to the very poor of the community, but in actuality communities are now so organized that such church membership patterns would be rare even where sought. Most sociologists find that most churches in a given community compete vigorously for "their slice of the pie" and all fail to show interest in marginal or peripheral elements of the community.

Modern community organization in the metropolis (where more and more people are coming to live) makes it impossible for the parish to be a unit which significantly cuts across lines of race and class. Michael Harrington has written of "The Other

America" made up of the poor, the diseased, the aged, the delinquent, the exploited, the bypassed racial groups. These are hidden from the view of the "affluent Americans" who build elevated trains or expressways over the Other America and in a thousand subtle ways find methods of neglecting it. When secular life is so organized, churches seldom break the pattern along parish lines. When significant portions of humanity are hidden from view in the antiseptic towns or suburbs where churches are, people also tend to lose their sense of empathy or sympathy for those who do not share their own kind of life. People in slum and suburb do not know, understand, or care for each other, and Christians in slum and suburb do not escape the pattern. Meanwhile other concerns — parish social life, the expense of building, the care for a good name — all serve to obscure the need for carrying on missionary and evangelistic work. (An aside to those readers of this book who are Lutheran: The most extensive survey yet taken of adult religious attitudes in America found that more than half of all adult Lutherans have *never* invited anyone to church and just over one fourth had succeeded when they invited someone. Conceiving of the church in the local community as a missionary resource center has not widely caught on in American Protestantism.)

The Question of Salvation

The result of the misplaced sense of mission and service is a widespread misconception of the purpose of the church in the world. The social analysts, joined by theologians, ask: What does this narrow, class-centered, grooved and clubby view of the religious institution do to the question of salvation? Indeed, if salvation means applying a slogan in question form ("Are you saved?") and an answer in slogan form ("Jesus saves!"); if salvation means hermetically sealing people in their baptismal water to wait for the Second Coming; if salvation means vacuum-packing

26

people in the parishes to save them for heaven someday — then salvation can be realized in parishes which have no sense of mission and service.

But if *Biblical* views of salvation are employed, then one cannot be content to speak of snatching a few people out of their environment and sustaining their morale by reference to a false picture of the real world around them. Biblical salvation, as the word in the Old Testament implies, includes ideas of wholeness, health, and enlargement of possibilities under the living God. Salvation involves asking who is saved from what for what by whom and to what end. Salvation includes working in the vineyard of the Lord; it means redeeming the time; it means inviting; it is involved with people who are saved for the world and sent into the world. The existence of the parish cannot be justified because it is the center where slogans are preached; they can be read by people who stay at home. Nor can it be justified because every doctrine there is guarded and kept intact; that can be done better away from people in the parishes. The parish has existed as the circle of disciples existed: to share and spread God's saving activity for all men. Until this is remembered, there is always the danger that one will consider himself justified not by the daring newness of God's act in Christ. He will be justified because he was wise enough to join the right religious club and prudent enough to keep its rules and regulations. The "outsider" then is not seen as someone who lives in the city over which Jesus weeps, who resides in the place where Christ is crucified and risen, whose sin causes that death but whose need motivates it; instead, the outsider is seen as the unwise and imprudent one who has not bothered to join the right religious club.

When the parish is inverted and concerned only about itself and its self-image, it is finally forced to create an unreal and trivial world inside the real one. Small goals are offered in place of large ones. The impression is created that if these smaller goals are met (meeting our budget, having our program advertised free in the newspapers, having our bazaar well attended), then the work of Christ in the world is advancing. This is not to say that the work of Christ is not made up of many small frustrations and successes but only to say that these smaller visions are part of a larger whole and must be kept in perspective. Churchmen today often bewail the secularism of life. No one contributes more to the secularization of life than people in parishes which in the name of sloganized salvation cut off their Christian vision from the basic decisions of their personal and public lives. The parish turned in upon itself often helps them cut themselves off from the world of decision.

What Do the Critics Prescribe?

This is not a book for professional social critics; it is not necessary here to detail in this brief space the findings of sociologists and theologians on which our brief summary has been based. Whoever is familiar with the scope of these studies will recognize here and there a summary line from the writings of a host of analysts: Obenhaus, Vidich, Bensman, Thomas, Greeley, Berger, Winter, Fairchild, Wynn, Kloetzli, Lenski, Sklare — this little gallery suggests the variety of people who help form such a composite. It seems to make little difference whether they are studying Protestant, Catholic, or Jew; rural, suburban, or urban settings; liberal or conservative denominations; whether they begin on Marxist or Weberian lines of interpretation. The results are sufficiently similar to suggest to us that today the social setting of parishes determines most of their public forms and moves — no matter how different their religious motivations and beliefs may be.

Some of these analysts and scholars make their study and then leave us in midair without advice or prescription. Strictly speaking, their discipline permits them to do this. If they announce

28

that they are going to do research and reporting we should not expect more than this. But quite often they do write a last chapter and let their religious concerns show in their vision of the future. We might say that when they fail to take a stand they are taking a stand; that is, failure to provide a plan implies that they believe the churches will learn from mere evidence. Some go a step further; Gerhard Lenski, for instance, will typically make his study and discuss the general trend. Then he will say, in effect: Now two or three choices are open to the churches. They can interrupt the trend or they can follow it; this depends on what knowledge they have and what attitudes they take as well as what desire and tenacity they possess.

Many go further than this. Some of the more radical (Hans Hoekendijk in Holland, Peter Berger and Gibson Winter in America) seem to be saying — and I hope this brevity does not result in caricature: "Let the old lady die." Let the parishes continue as burial societies, religious clubs, and — at best — centers for liturgy and preaching. But do not invest new energy or hope in them. If people want to be part of them, let them know that their sense of Christian mission and service will be dimmed there, that they are embarking on a precarious Christian vocation — much as if they were going to a monastery. But divert the world's attention and the churches' best energies from them so that something new can emerge.

Not all such radical critics specify what these emergent forms may be. Some of them speak of highly technical forms of ministry in factories, to labor unions, to leaders of racial revolution. Others speak of "lay academies," where laymen of special vision and energy will relate Christ to their jobs and their leisure. Some turn with hope to the mass media of communications or to a campus ministry. Most of them look with some hope to "house churches," to smaller cells of concerned Christians meeting away from the institutional setting. Still others say, in effect, that God and history will provide us with as yet unanticipated forms if only we will be open to what He has to offer. But our parishes close us off from being open and creative.

Strong words, these. Easy words to dismiss, they are, if we accept them as the acid directions of sour critics. But what do we make of them when by their words and works the critics show that they do have the best interests of Christ's work at heart? Of course, they may be wrong, dead wrong. If so, this must be shown more effectively than it has been. Either their methods are wrong and faulty, or their samples are inaccurate, or they are cheating or engaging in false reporting. Most vulnerable of all would be their subjective conclusions and prescriptions. But what if they are proved to be largely correct?

The Reactions of Church People in Parishes

Many reactions are open among church people who begin to get the point. Sometimes the studies are greeted in panic and without the perspective history gives. Yes, God seems almost to have "written off" whole epochs and locations of the church in the past as far as the carrying on of His work among men is concerned. Perhaps our time is such an epoch and our place such a location when and where the forms we create are barriers to His speaking and acting among men. But often out of a "written off" area and in an unpromising time He has, through His servants and prophets, brought about newness and birth. If the social analysts awaken us to be ready for such devastation and birth, they will have filled a function more important than that which they adopt when they bring in their prescriptions.

Sometimes churches react in panic and are paralyzed into immobility. Sometimes church people use these studies and findings as an excuse not to become further involved and committed to their suffering for Christ in the world and in the church. Young people have sometimes found them an excuse for dismissing in impatience all religious institutions and to set themselves pride-fully above the prosaic struggles of others. Others will look for minor exceptions that will temporarily justify the existence of the parishes or will seek to justify them (as well they might) on some other grounds than those of mission and service. They may legitimately point to areas of mission and service which were overlooked by the generalizer. But the more thoughtful people are haunted by the question: What if the analyst and critics are right and we should work for wholly new forms? What if the parishes should die off to make room for new creations that will better equip people for Christian service and mission?

When Pastors Respond

Now let us look at the pastoral side of the response. Again, we shall take an instance of highest motivation and faithful fulfill-ment. A pastor, let us say, has heard, read, and listened to the critics. He has tried to revise his thinking and his parish's life in the light of what he has learned. The beginnings of the effects of these studies has been evident in some circles of clergy and informed laity. Many parishes have begun to be responsive and to revise; unfortunately, they do not always receive the attention they deserve. But the good parson also has ground of his own whereon to stand.

Has the social analyst, in his desire to look at the whole, neglected the part? Is he misusing the role of the person? Mission and service are not abstractions, ideal "things" to be imposed on the church. They refer to specific people who are to be saved, healed, made whole, given directions, given enlargement of their possibilities. Mission and service are designed to bring people into the kind of orbit where the pastoral kind of activity is mean-ingful. Sometimes the social analyst, for example, reveals an anti-middle-class bias. He speaks disparagingly of the way the white American Christian of middle income and moderate education

31

lives. He complains of the lack of opportunity which slum dwellers or migratory workers share. When he is asked to spell out the physical side of "the good life" for those bypassed by middle-class life, he proposes "a fair shake" for them which looks and sounds very much like the affluent life situation he had been decrying.

Sometimes the critics overlook the role of religion in helping people be "integrated" with their environment. Some parishes do a creditable task in bringing people into contact with a workable-size group of others and in helping all develop a Christian way of looking at person and world. God's missionaries and servants are to see their work in tension with their environment, for earth as it is is not the fulfilled kingdom of God, and preaching of the Law is necessary. But their work is not only in tension with the environment. They should also help people find positive ways of living in and using the resources of the world, and renewed parishes can help do this.

Others of pastoral heart and vision will question the strategy of the analysts. Are they being overdramatic in their generalizations, overlooking some good things which do happen in exceptional circumstances? If good things can happen, is it wise to kill off forms and pull away from them before something rather concrete appears to summon the energies and loyalties of hundreds of millions of people? Have the analysts, by concentrating chiefly on the public sphere, overlooked the importance of the hiddenness of much Christian life? This life cannot be advertised; it disintegrates into prideful attention-getting or embarrassment when it is publicly noticed. But every pastor is encouraged to see evidences of such quiet service even in routine parishes. What will happen to these evidences if energies are wholly diverted from parishes?

Are the critics in the best position to bring prescription? They, too, are conditioned by their culture in their universities and with their professional standards. Are we so sure the church would be better off in "emergent forms of service"? Or could it be that these would fall into the hands of prideful people who would be developing a new kind of bureaucracy, a new kind of club, a sort of pseudochurch alongside the real one? Don't these miss the exceptional circumstances, such as the instances where a parish pastor is more effective in, say, a freedom march because he has to report back to a group of people who may have to be changed in order to understand what he has done? The academic man finds his activity in such controversial fronts to be uncontroversial; he does not have to report back and bring others around to his vision or standard.

The man of pastoral vision asks whether the analysts are impatient with history. Are they looking for the Great Design that will remove people from the compromises and frustrations of daily life? Is there perhaps a sense of "neatness" that leads them to want to kill off the existing institutions or to let them die? Can these not be transformed? Do not the critics work with a picture of a "Golden Age" of past or future and thus do they not resist the present with its mundane and humdrum character?

Finally, dare one let a "sociology of the church" define a "theology of the church"? Christians have learned to take their definitions first from the commands and promises of God. We have agreed that the mandates or commands concerning parish life are very few in number. But when these are directly affected, they cannot be bypassed or abandoned because they seem inefficient or because they violate the neatness a social thinker or theologian might seek.

So pastors and lay leaders reveal a variety of reactions. They may remain ignorant of the findings; they may avoid them; they may refute them. They may learn from them by undertaking critical questioning themselves. They may learn and adapt with new forms. They may learn half a lesson and abandon the whole cause. They may learn and await the new where they are. To such pastors the views of the social analysts are basically correct but they are only part of the picture and their credentials for bringing in prescription are not as creditable as are their credentials for bringing diagnosis.

What Is Needed for New Birth? Eighteen Steps

In such a situation the authors of this book suggest that a definition of death and birth in the church may be one way beyond the stalemate. Scripture provides a few mandates and a few more patterns; nothing else. From there on we are "free agents" to listen to tradition and to work with the best in our own contemporary environments. If parishes are killed or if they die, what elements must reappear? As we see it, whatever appears must witness to faith in a Father who redeems through the work of His Son and in the power of the Spirit. This Trinity must be matched by a trinity among men: the presence of Jesus and at least two other people, which is the mathematical beginning of the picture of the church in Matthew. These trinities are brought together in activity of witness in the Word. This witness springs from a read Scripture with the Spirit working through the Word, from heard preaching, from uttered and unuttered intercession, from mutual upbuilding through Christian conversation. It takes material form in "a loaf of bread, a bottle of wine, and a river" or some other form of their elements — the only ones needed for a full expression of the material side of Christian worship. The witness and sustenance issue in works of love, which are the evidence of the presence of faith; for we now have a community in time, working while it is day. But there is also a sense of community in place. This group of people has gathered here and not there; it exists in this environment. It may exist only momentarily and may almost every day be made up of a somewhat different group of people. But there is some sense of "place-ness," some bond with environment and responsibility to the immediate setting. We cannot find much more in the Biblical sources except the suggestions that these activities be "ordered" and given some sense of permanence.

All the rest — buildings, budgets, programs, voluntary organizations — grow out of and are judged by the minimum implied in the Biblical mandate and reality. This is not to say that institutions are unimportant. Christianity knows in one sense no "noninstitutional" church. Institutions are so important that they deserve most searching scrutiny. Since this book discusses death and birth of the parish and not "new and emerging forms of ministry," we shall focus finally on what such a view would do to local congregations, since they do survive and prevail and probably shall do so in some cultural form or other. What kinds of results for the local parish are implied in the picture if new birth is a possibility? The other authors will detail some of these in specific settings; I shall speak in general terms.

If local congregations are to continue in existence in the modern world, they will have to look at the world itself as a problem. If they wish to devise mission to that world in a way which will make any use or sense of parishes, it will only be if they develop a sense of interdependence. Denominationally and ecumenically each parish will have to undertake a basic inquiry about its own purpose and mission in the light of its own environment and its contribution to the world mission of the church.

The theological parallel of this first strategic word is this: just as parishes are interdependent, so they are dependent. Logically (first in place of order) and chronologically (first in place of time) *the* church is prior to and basic to its local manifestations. Just as "independistic" views will not serve strategy, so they will not serve understanding. Every move a local congregation makes must be made in the light of its small part in the whole church in the world.

The standards for measuring the meaning of the local church come chiefly from outside the local community in the Word of God and in the whole human condition. The local community will usually provide standards to which the parish has already begun to conform, because it has helped form them, and compromise has gone on and will continue from there.

People do act on "images" which they carry of reality. Interdependent and dependent parishes will learn that health of one at the expense of another will not contribute to the image of health and vitality of the whole church. What is said or done in a parish in Birmingham, Ala., has a great deal to do with the kinds of decision made in Detroit, and vice versa. This means that congregations not located at strategic crossroads have to think and act in such a way so as, at least, not to complicate the life of churches which are so located.

Parishes must be content to think of themselves as a Christian "presence" in the world, whether or not they are immediately and obviously productive in their environment. This will help the stronger ones not to apply false standards to those which are in less productive environments. For decades the churches must be "present" in the inner city or on the campus, without having the burden of fulfilling certain statistical expectations. American suburban churches thus dare not apply their standards to European churches or to gatherings in New Guinea.

If parishes are to survive and to play a part in the emerging lines of the church, the utmost simplicity must accompany their actions. In a technical world their forms will inevitably grow more complicated and technical than is desirable. But a parish that walks in newness of life can daily and weekly subject its forms to the canons of simplicity and economy. The parish does not have to do everything and be everything in the world. It need not have a miniature reproduction of every element of the world

36

applied now to its members, such as all the forms of leisure and social life.

Each parish, if it is to have a legitimate existence, will work to minister to the center of people's lives instead of the tangents. If it works only with their private and family lives, it must reach to the central human needs; where it reaches public dimensions of existence, it must provide an interpretation of life and history which will inform all that is done. The typical overly busy parish contents itself with touching the many edges of peoples' lives, entertaining them or occupying them in trivial tasks. What they need and deserve from a Christian ministry is a basic way of looking at what life and eternity demand and offer them.

So long as parishes are to play a part in the economy of the church in the modern world, they will have to adapt to the great mobility of people. Meaningless variety, idiosyncrasy, institutional eccentricity — these do not well serve people who move frequently from place to place and must undertake servanthood where they are, immediately.

Parishes that are dependent on the church and interdependent with other parishes and institutions will ordinarily cooperate with other parishes everywhere in whatever ways are compatible with their central theological vision. Today parishes compete not only across denominational lines but even within denominations, because they are measured by an implicit statistical standard of success. Thus too often they fail to rejoice in one another's victories or share one another's burdens.

They will work to reestablish a sense of discipline, but this discipline will concentrate less on "the rules of the club" and more on the meaning of Christian discipleship.

If parishes are to survive or, better, to die and be reborn, they will orient their evangelism first to the marginal elements of the community and let those predisposed to join "find" the church.

Budgets should also be reoriented to first take care of other needs beyond the local.

Parishes will reorganize so that their activities will be seen to flow from one center and so that they will not seem to be meaningless, patternless mosaics of irrelevant and unrelated activities.

Parishes will have to become "lay academies" for the training of a sort of "elite corps" or core of Christian workers. Lay retreats in such congregations would concentrate less on churchmanship and more on "worldmanship"; less on "how to be an usher" and more on "Christ and my job."

Such parishes or units would learn how to define themselves in minimum terms, without extravagant claims. Many, many Christian tasks are not well suited to their means. Parish leaders will learn to measure Christian activity in other ways than counting "how many nights a week we have the members busy on the premises."

Parishes of new birth would work with social analysts to develop emergent ministries, to help new forms of church life to be born. They will contribute personnel, funds, and understanding for their development.

Metropolitan churches will see that their destiny and their mission are one; it is impossible to have a permanently healthy unit in an area of permanent general disease in the body of Christ in the modern city.

If such congregations are to be born, they will free their professional servants for "emergent" and "emergency" tasks rather than to demand of them that they fulfill many trivial roles culturally associated with ministry.

They may do all of this, and the church in our epoch and place may still fail to see enlarged the reconciling circle of God's activity. But such failure would be a part of the limits of man's

38

finitude then, and not of his foolishness. Churches should remove some of the offenses of their irrelevance. At present the rural church often looks like the Grange, a sort of fraternal society that has passed its peak; it still holds loyalties, but who must really reckon with it? Urban churches often look like corner delicatessens in a day of supermarkets and chains — like competitive little enterprises in a day when people are more than ever before interactive and interdependent. Churches in their local forms can at least be revised and reborn — to stand ready should the Spirit, who comes as He wills and as the wind blows, choose to utilize them for the reconciling activity of Jesus Christ in a diseased and dying world.

"For the form of this world is passing away." (1 Cor. 7:31)

"And He who sat upon the throne said, "Behold, I make all things new." (Rev. 21:5)

Notes

1. Robert O. Blood and Donald M. Wolfe, *Husbands and Wives* (Glencoe, Ill.: The Free Press, 1960).

2. Robert Heilbroner, "On the Seriousness of the Future," *The American Scholar*, XXXII (Autumn 1963), 557, 559.

Death and Birth of the Parish

IN TOWN AND COUNTRY

Paul R. Biegner

✠

Death and Birth of the Parish

❧

IN TOWN AND COUNTRY

"Small Enough to Know You, Large Enough to Serve You" or some variation thereof is the highway sign that greets you. As you adjust to the 30-mile-an-hour speed zone, you note the "marks of small-town America — the cluster of little stores huddled up against one another as if for mutual protection against the . . . monster supermarket on the edge of town, the volunteer fire company, the Legion Hall, and four Protestant churches regarding one another fiercely from the four corners of the main intersection. . . . It looks much as it did 30 or 40 years ago, but overlaid with the color and symbol of contemporary America." [1]

Except for greater prosperity the outer appearance is one of little change, with all at peace and harmony. This is deceptively false. Town and country America is caught between two worlds; it is threatened and confused by drastic change.

A LOOK AT TOWN AND COUNTRY AMERICA TODAY

The 1960 U. S. Census defined both "town and country" and "rural" as referring to villages and towns of 2,500 or less, and included open country, crossroads, hamlets, and rural townships having a population of 2,500 or less. However, we make an exception to the census definition to include small cities up to 10,000 population. Unless adjacent to standard metropolitan statistical areas of 50,000 population or more, most 10,000 population communities and churches will show heavy rural influence and stamp of character. "Town and Country" and "rural" are used interchangeably.

Greater Agricultural Productivity

What Winston Churchill said of Britain's airmen during World War II also applies to American farmers: "Never did so many owe so much to so few." Never before in history has such a small percent of the total population provided a nation's food and fibre.

The average American farmworker 100 years ago produced enough food and fibre to support fewer than five persons; his modern counterpart supplies the needs of nearly 30. In the last 40 years — since only 1920 — an agricultural revolution has increased farm output per hour 400%. The combination of better practices, increased yields, and fewer man-hours per acre meant an overall decline from 119 to 22 man-hours per 100 bushels of corn between 1920 and 1959. While milk production per cow averaged 4,000 pounds in 1920, it had grown to 6,071 by 1959, with man-hours needed to produce a hundredweight of milk declining from 3.6 to 1.9.

This breakthrough in farm production has been due to scientific advance and increased applications of technology and mechanization. Acreage did not greatly increase. Man-hours declined drastically. The answer is to be found in new hybrid breeds of corn, new ways of feeding cattle and hogs, new forms of fertilizer, new methods of irrigation and pest control, new machinery, wider capital investment, and the application of business management and cost accounting to farming.

Two far-reaching agricultural revolutions have come in quick succession. In the 1920s horses and oats grown by the farmer were replaced by tractors, self-propelled combines, and petroleum. The second revolution, in progress for the last decade or two (but greatly accelerated in the past few years), is the undergirding of farm production and marketing with vast amounts of science, technology, and business management. As farmers could produce ✓ more with less labor, they were able to operate larger farms. Those who made that step found that investment for land, buildings, and equipment grew from $6,094 in 1940 to $33,455 by 1959. In short, agriculture has changed within 40 years from a traditional way of life to a way of making a living.

In terms of greater productivity and efficiency and long-range progress, it is wrong to think of agriculture as declining. We do not think of the airlines as a declining industry just because a pilot in a jet airliner can now take 125 passengers from Chicago to New York in two hours, compared with 40 passengers in eight hours, 20 years ago. Agriculture, like airlines, is a strong and ✓ growing industry. Dr. Earl L. Butz, Dean of Agriculture at Purdue University says that although American agriculture is making extensive economic and sociological adjustments, there is a bright future ahead for the able and ambitious, well capitalized farmer with sufficient volume of business for an economic operating unit.

Static or Declining Income

From the viewpoint of the city dweller or suburbanite the American consumer works fewer hours to feed himself and his family. Only 20 cents out of each take-home dollar goes to buy a balanced and varied diet. The average American industrial worker was able in 1960 to buy much more food with his take-home wage than in 1947—49: 54% more pork, 32% more beef, 21% more potatoes, 62% more peas, and 100% more eggs.

The success of American agriculture has brought full market baskets to the consumer, but often a cost/price squeeze to the American farmer. Declines in prices received for their products and increases in prices they paid for fertilizers, machinery, and plant improvement meant that farmers have much less net income than nonfarm people.

The 1960 U. S. census revealed that the median family earnings in 1959 for the entire United States stood at $4,595; however, farmers' and farm managers' families stood at $2,136, while farm laborers' families' median income was only $1,107. On an individual basis, urban median income in 1959 was $1,532 with rural farm income less than half of that, $731, and rural non-farm income $942. By 1959 only 13% of U. S. families had income less than $2,000, while nearly half (43%) received from $5,000 to $10,000. However, families headed by farm operators or farm laborers comprised 39% of the families with less than $2,000 of income, even though these farm families comprised only 8% of all U. S. families in 1960.

Since 1947—49 the prices received for agricultural commodities fell 12% while costs of production rose 12%; thus profits were cut a total of 24%. During 1952—60, prices paid by farmers rose 4% but prices received fell 18%; net farm income fell from about $15,000,000,000 to $11,000,000,000 in 1960.

While these cost/price pressures squeeze all farmers, those especially hurt are the "traditional farmers" who have been by-passed by the sweeping social and economic changes of the past generation. The traditional farmer is often an older man, who has been stung by the depression; he does not look at farming as a way of making a living but as a traditional way of life. He survives by cutting investment and costs and by operating with secondhand machinery in limited quantities. Some machinery may have been in use for 20 to 40 years. In a period of declining prices he combines "low fixed operating costs and marginal consumption standards" to avert the cost/price squeeze. Government economists estimate that "traditional farmers" number from ¾ of a million to 1¾ million working on marginal or submarginal operations.[2]

Economic and Social Insecurity

Agriculture's success has led to agriculture's distress. Prosperous farmers who have adapted to the technological advances of farming science and engineering have in some cases paid a high social cost. Gone is the placid way of life half idealized and half remembered from their childhood; instead some complain about "the rat race" as family farms grow even larger, investment needs continue to mushroom, and farming becomes more specialized.

Even more insecure are the traditional farmers. Government economists talk freely of "wide underemployment" existing in agriculture since 90% of current production could be maintained by only 40% of those now engaged in farming. The Committee of Economic Development, a private organization of business and industrial leaders, recently recommended moving ½ million substandard farmers out of farming each year. The planners agree that the number of farmers must decrease. While an average farmer can produce for 30 or more now, consumers' stomachs are still relatively inelastic, and human backs are only so broad.

Uneven development and adoption of farm practices has caused serious dislocation among small and traditional farmers in some areas. Every technological advance creates wider demands for highly skilled operators with managerial ability and eagerness. This leaves the increasing numbers with limited skills outstripped and unable to adjust. Even in good farming areas there are traditional farmers with low income. Some have made a sort of adjustment by taking nonfarm jobs; they drive school buses, haul milk, or work in a factory or garage in town. They may take the job either as a way of building up capital to enter farming full time or as a more or less permanent way of life.

The farmer in this process of transition pays a high cost. In halfway deciding it's not worth it, he may decide to take a job, work an 8-hour shift, but continue to farm on the side of a scale commensurate with his ability and energy. Such coexistence is seldom peaceful; the traditional farmer loves his way of life; his family is accustomed to that way of life. His fatigue from the factory and his inability to farm as he could cause frustration and deepen the inner feeling of failure. His sense of failure becomes more acute when his wife has to work in a store in town or a nearby city factory; she is earning the bread instead of baking it. In the past surplus farm labor was needed by other sectors of the economy. Now through further applications of mechanization and through automation, opportunities for nonskilled or semiskilled labor are shrinking continually.

Widespread insecurity may be found among many prosperous farmers who nervously follow the projections of agricultural experts. For example, the U. S. Department of Agriculture recently released an estimate that for the American farmer to retain his share of the nation's economic growth, where in 1960 three and one half farm families were directly engaged in agriculture there would have to be only one farm family by the year 2,000. Economic pressures that force the small, inadequate farmers to stop farming may by extension crowd out the medium-size farmer later on. No one likes to be expelled from a traditional way of life by economic and social forces too big for him to control.

The farmer who enjoys his way of life would like to be able to have his children follow in his footsteps but finds it economically impossible. A youth who belongs to the Future Farmers of America told me, "Probably less than two out of 10 of our chapter members will ever own a farm, and then only if we inherit it." During a 10-year period from 1945 to 1954, on a nationwide basis 31% of the farms were vacated by retiring farmers. Yet only 16% were available for beginners; the other 15% were merged with enlarged farm operations. Surveys have shown that in typical rural areas in the Corn Belt approximately one farm per township per year will become available for a new farm operator. In those same townships, the number of farm youth ready for farm employment each year ranges from four to eight. Obviously not all can remain on the farm.

The farm revolution has given farm laborers an even stiffer

jolt. The traditional hired man close to the farmer's family is being displaced by "migrants and machine tenders in the fields and in the dairy." Landlessness has become a reality. Rootless and landless sharecroppers and tenants, landless migratory workers, and landless southern Negroes have grown in direct proportion to the reach of mechanization.[3]

Declining Population

Rural areas have slimmed down while fattening the cities and suburbs. While most urban areas are growing rapidly, never before in the United States have so many rural areas declined in population. Fifty metropolitan counties, each having more than 50,000 population, gained the equivalent of 50% of the total national increase from 1950 to 1960. The United States has 3,134 counties. Though only 361 are entirely or partly included in metropolitan areas and number less than 12% of all counties, 84% of the nation's total growth in the 1950s occurred within them. The vast town and country reaches grew at the rate of only 7.5%. In view of this concentrated growth it is little surprise that almost half (49%) of the counties actually declined in population. In general the 1960 census showed that the rural population declined rapidly in the heavily agricultural areas, but town and country areas near cities of 50,000 or more absorbed a near equivalent number of rural nonfarm people.

The accelerated movement to cities and suburbs can be marked by a swift backward glance. Until 75 years ago America was predominately a rural society and an agricultural economy. Today it is neither. Even while frontier lands were still opening at the time of the first industrial revolution the percentage of farmers was already dropping. Around 1825 some three fourths of the gainfully employed Americans were farm-employed; by 1875 the percentage had dropped to one half. Presently some 9% of the 70 million Americans in the labor force live on the farm; but only 4.3 million of the nearly 7 million are in the category of the independent farmer on the family-size farm. Studies by the Department of Labor predict that the number of workers in agriculture will continue to decline — with a further 17% decline by 1970 projected.

Decline in Small Town's Vitality

Somewhere in the quarter century between 1935 and 1955 a decisive turn was made away from small-town life. Max Lerner observes: "The currents of American energy moved around and beyond the small town, leaving them isolated and demoralized, with their young people leaving them behind like abandoned ghost towns."

Much of this decline is due to town and country areas losing their economic base. This has already occurred in some areas badly scarred by soil erosion and mining of soil resources. In others marginal land has been placed into the soil bank, or mining and timbering have declined. Lerner concludes:

> Everywhere, even in the most prosperous areas, the small town was undercut by the big changes in American life — the auto and superhighway, the supermarket and the market center, the mail-order house, the radio and TV, the growth of national advertising, the mechanization of farming — so that it turned its face directly to the centers of technology.[4]

Small hamlets whose excuse for existence has been wiped out find that improved all-weather roads and highways further constrict the trade areas from which they can draw sustenance. Improved roads only accelerate their decline. The highway, with its invitations to bypass and ignore the villages it avoids, deepens a trend already under way: larger towns will continue to grow and villages will wither.

Most small towns in strictly farming areas have been hit hard by this decline. A drive down main street will find many store windows staring vacantly. New investment in public buildings or business is almost nil. Old Doc, the general practitioner, closes his office when he retires and the door stays locked since no younger man wants to take the practice. Businesses closely linked to the expansion necessary for modern farming hold their own by adding new lines of machinery, seed and feed additives, fertilizer, fuel, and power. Retail services slump as more town and country people go to larger towns or the big city for convenience shopping, specialized shopping, and professional services.

Small-town merchants operate in an atmosphere of scarcity. They avoid products with no established market or wide demand. Much of their clientele becomes limited to the loyal, the aged, and those forced to buy on credit. As the larger cities continue their drawing power and as the tentacles of the mail-order house reach out wider and wider, the small-town merchant loses a greater volume of business. To compete he cuts costs and lengthens store hours. However, the attraction of superior marketing, processing, and farm services offered in metropolitan areas continues to grow.

Loss of Decision-Making Power

The traditional town and country view of the city is a combination of grudging admiration and personal aversion: "The city is a good place to visit, but I sure would hate to live there." This expresses more than a distaste for the overwhelming massiveness of great buildings or the confusion of bewildering traffic patterns and expressways. Rather the town and country dweller recoils instinctively from the awesome power of the city. In the giant city decisions are made that affect the entire country and sometimes the entire world. America's power is wielded today by the business complexes. Often raw power rests in the ham-like fists of labor leaders like Jimmy Hoffa, or in illegal manipulations of narcotics, gambling, and white slavery by big crime. Pressure groups and pitchmen shape their message to America via mass media from the concrete canyons of the city. Knowing this we may

51

forget that in yesteryear the decisions that expressed the American mind were largely made by the small-town lawyers, bankers, merchants, and editors.

Town and country areas find themselves tied down politically by large school subsidies — many of them from urban areas. National politics end at the county and state levels, bypassing the small towns. Out of this antagonism and reluctant admiration come the court battles over reapportionment or the traditional urban-rural hostility, which pits upstate New York versus New York City or downstate Illinois against Chicago.

Small Town Life Falsely Idealized

Like the fading beauty queen who reminisces over beauty contests won 25 years before, so the small town often reads its own clippings so long that it deludes itself into believing them still to be true. That the small town is still surrounded by wistful admirers from the big city and sprawling suburb only deepens a mutual self-deception.

Town and country people have a falsely idealized image of themselves and their society. Because rural areas are no longer provincially isolated but employ modern techniques and products coming from the cities, town and country people feel they can combine the advantages of both urban and rural life without the disadvantages of either. They insist they are still "just plain folks." Vidich and Bensman illuminate this idealized point of view and false image in their classic, *Small Town in Mass Society*. They list these illusions:

1. That the basic traditions of American society — "grassroots democracy," free and open expression, individualism — are most firmly located in rural society. The American heritage is better preserved in the small town because it can resist bad city influences and thereby preserve the best of the past.

2. That the future hope of American society lies in rural life because it has resisted all "isms" and constitutes the only major bulwark against them.

52

3. That much of the progress of society is the result of rural talent which has migrated to the cities. In this way rural society has a positive influence on urban life; rural migrants account for the virtues of city life. . . .

4. That "when you live in a small town you can take or leave the big cities — go there when you want to and always come back without having to live as they do." There is the belief that "if more people lived in small towns, you wouldn't have all those problems." [5]

The fact that the small town is dwindling in economic, social, and political importance makes urban Americans idealize it all the more.

The phrase "small town" has come itself to carry a double layer of meaning, at once sentimental and condescending. There is still a belief that democracy is more idyllic at the "grass roots," that the business spirit is purer, that the middle class is more intensely middling. There is also a feeling that by the fact of being small the small town somehow escapes the corruptions of life in the city and the dominant contagions that infest the more glittering places. [6]

This yearning for the tranquility and rural simplicity of the small town is apparently a nostalgic search for some social pattern which we could better manage than the sprawling strip-cities and urban-suburban constellations. The small town cannot be propped up; it will not again assume the vitality or growth it had 50 years ago.

Perhaps the nostalgia never really had any basis except in the dream of some ideal shape of communal living. Anyone who has taken a hard look under the surface of small-town life will have realized the basic self-deception. Heartbreaking inertia, resistance to anything but the soporificly familiar, the wide prevalence of moneygrubbing, pursuit of pleasure or leisure or the buck, keeping up with the Joneses, the unwillingness to stick your neck out, the cancer of corruption and greed — all are present in town and country. While there might be greater simplicity and surface tranquility in the small town, few can say that there is more happiness. While people may know and greet one another on the small-town street, many of them are lost and bewildered, looking to "whatness" rather than "whoness" — for security and for purpose in life.

Pessimistic Amid Loss of Community

The 1-room school house with peeling paint and choking weeds and the sagging roof line of a country church are silent reminders of the loss of community. Now casualties to rapid change, they once served as community centers. In the early days of our history, schools, churches, and stores were dotted over the countryside to serve people whose mode of transportation was the horse. No longer does every crossroads hamlet or village serve as community center. All-weather roads and the auto make it easy for small-town residents to drive to one of the larger towns for services.

On the urban fringe rapid change forces interdependence upon reluctant rural areas. Rapid growth gets things out of kilter, as people find that old established ways of doing things don't work as well. A fairly self-sufficient small town may be forced into radical readjustment when it suddenly finds itself catapulted into close orbit around the big city. Old loyalties and community ties keep washing away when people live in a small town, work in a larger town or city, and purchase much of their clothing, raw materials, and other specialties in still a third. People on the urban fringe may drive 25 to 40 miles to jobs in the city; a growing number may drive 50 or more miles. To understand the extent of this development the 1960 census notes that 4.2 million persons or 24% of the total rural labor force was employed in manufacturing, as compared to 3.8 million persons or 22% who were farming. In 1950, just 10 years earlier, farming's proportion was twice that of manufacturing — 36% and 18% respectively. Small towns around bigger cities will have growth problems — growth caused by the economic attraction and stimulation

54

of businesses and residents whose work is related to the large metropolitan city.

Problems of decline and of growing or already profound pes-√ simism meet the declining or static community. While other areas are growing rapidly, a community may be standing still or moving backward. Old-timers remember vividly the period when the community was still thriving. Painful reminders of the decline can be seen almost daily in the frequent farm auctions, the empty farmhouses, the deteriorating mansions of old aristocrats, and the notices in the paper of sales of estates.

This trend is likely to continue for quite some time. Of the more than 3,000 counties in the United States, there are 991 counties with no population center larger than 2,500 and another 1,176 counties with population centers ranging from 2,500 to 10,000. However, a great deal of growth has occurred in smaller centers from 5,000 to 10,000 population, from 10,000 to 25,000 population, and from 25,000 to 50,000 population. The 1960 census indicated significant population and economic growth during the 50s in these areas; they grew at the rate of 19.4, 47.9, and 69.2%, respectively. Villages, small towns, and rural areas are steadily losing their future, as young people between the ages of 18 and 30 (the age bracket in which the highest rate of migration occurs) move to urban America for jobs or further training in college or technical institutes. In communities heavily weighted with elderly and middle-aged people, young children decline in number. While nationally in 1959 there were two and one half times more births than deaths, in the 1960s the number of heavily agricultural counties having more deaths than births is likely to increase "substantially."

Homogenized Through Mass Culture

The process of "rurbanization" [7] is altering town and country life in vast segments of our country. In countless communities a homogenization process is in progress as urban and rural communities meet and intermingle within commuting distance of larger centers. Many younger families and older urban people have taken advantage of all-weather roads, REA, the consolidated school, and the school bus and have made the move into town and country areas, making the rural nonfarm population the most mobile segment in the 1960 census.

This is a two-way flow. Rural families often have one or more members commuting to the city for work; the farmer does his shopping and trading less in the village and more in the larger industrial center, where machinery, parts, new cars, and the J. C. Penney version of the newest fashions can be secured for his wife and daughter. The car, radio, TV, and movies, "the standardizing forces of American culture," as Lerner terms them, have brought the rural population out of isolation. The city limits sign at the edge of the county seat or regional large town no longer symbolizes wide cultural or social cleavage between rural and urban. The same sort of people live on both sides of that city limits sign, sharing the same communications, electricity, church, education, and transportation.

While urban and rural life mingle and merge on the rurban fringe of the larger town, the static or declining rural areas far removed by distance from direct mixing with urban life are becoming more ingrown. This is true even though static and declining rural areas share urban mass media. Those younger people who have found it more difficult to adjust are the very first to leave for the larger towns or big cities. The steady migration of young folks to college and big-city jobs and the small number of "outsiders" that static or declining communities attract make them far less exposed to people from other areas importing deviant attitudes, values, and ways of life.

Riesman in *The Lonely Crowd* detects a growing tendency for people to be "other-directed" rather than "inner-directed."

The majority no longer are predominately pioneers and individualists, but constantly rotate invisible antennas to pick up signals from those around them; an inner process of feedback alters their behavior and character according to patterns that they observe among their peers. As a result of low inmigration the peer group in static or declining rural areas is usually the larger family unit. James H. Coop, associate professor of rural sociology at Pennsylvania State University, cites a survey of a static Pennsylvania small town:

> Analysis of origins of people in one Pennsylvania rural community showed that in 75% of the households one or both spouses grew up in the community. Of the remaining 25% two thirds had close relatives living within the community. Only 4% of the 613 households could be classified as newcomers who had lived in the community less than 10 years and had no kinship ties within the community.
>
> No doubt the closeness of kinship ties tends to stabilize the values and norms held by people in the community. Deviant behavior cannot be cloaked with anonymity; the censure of kin is an ever present reality.[8]

Riesman's parody of the nursery rhyme holds true for isolated rural areas also: "all little pigs go to market; none stay home; all have roast beef, if any do; and all say 'we-we.' "[9]

As iron filings are involuntarily drawn into a magnetic field, so the vast rural areas are feeling the increasing influence of the metropolitan clusters — with mixed results. On the plus side, town and country areas are no longer isolated and excessively provincial but are sharing ever more widely in America's mass culture. Negatively, the far-reaching economic and social changes, widely feared and only half understood, have brought in their train social shock and dislocation; these all too often are only half-heartedly confronted by people who are insecure, confused, and pessimistic. Further, in the midst of agricultural plenty and in spite of increased efficiency and additional applications of agricultural technology, farm areas are faced with declining income and shrinking profit margins. The vast town and country stretches between metropolitan centers can be sure that the following trends will continue into the foreseeable future:

(1) The number of full-time farmers will continue to decline. (2) New residents in rural areas will not be farmers; their ways and thoughts will not be "our" ways and thoughts. (3) While fringe areas close to metropolitan centers will experience spurts of growth, small-town areas 70 miles or more from these centers will barely hold their own or decline in vigor and size.

WHAT MUST DIE IN THE TOWN AND COUNTRY PARISH

In God's plan the church is people — people whose life-source is Christ: "I am the Vine, you are the branches." The church is God's living organism, planted and sustained by the daily experience of His grace and not by the pressures of environment. As an organism that lives and grows in Christ, the church differs fundamentally from organizations both as to inner life and outer purpose. The church is God's vine, the plant which the risen Christ by His Spirit daily prunes and cleanses with the forgiving word. Union with the risen Christ for His purposes in the world is the basis for the initial call, the continuation, and the conclusion: "Dwell in Me, as I in you." So the church, confronting social shock and change, should take its structure and shape from God's steadiness of purpose, not from any assumed permanence of social or economic conditions.

Town and country parishes differ widely: some are experiencing growth on the urban fringe, while many have a declining rural population; some have known progressive and stable pastoral and lay leadership, while others have suffered through long vacancies and little vision. But the basic contrast between parishes is not decided by external factors such as environment, numerical size, or the age, wealth, or influence of membership, but is decided by understanding and living out God's plan for the church.

Some parishes can not only articulate a good understanding of their God-given purpose but have actually lived that out. Far too many parishes, like Willie Loman in *Death of a Salesman,* never knew who they were, having only the vaguest notion of who called them into existence and why. Such betrayals of God's purpose, sidetracking the parish from its purpose and mission-service as church, deserve the most rigorous and relentless criticism. Radical repentance is needed not only by fallen individuals sorry for having been on the wrong track; rural parishes must repent radically for failure to be what they are — God's church.

Ethelbert Stauffer calls the church from its reveling in self-congratulation and self-deception to a radical repentance that will result in a rethinking and reliving of the church and its mission:

> But what is the temptation to which the church is exposed in history? It is the temptation to pious self-glorification, the same temptation to which the synagogue succumbed. . . . This temptation meets the church in a thousand different forms, a thousand different dangers threaten her mission, dangers by comparison with which all the threats to her stability are entirely secondary. . . . The church no longer has her desire set upon her Lord, but upon her own piety. She says: 'I am rich, and have gotten riches, and have need of nothing' — but does not know that she is pitiable and destitute, and poor and blind and empty (Rev. 3:17; cf. Matt. 23:15, 30). The church becomes too important in her own estimation. She safeguards her historical existence instead of justifying it. . . . She holds her form to be more important than her mission, and takes her dogmatics more seriously than her God. . . . The place where God's honour dwells becomes a breeding place of pious titles (Mark 12:38 f.; Matt. 23:8 ff.). The 'we' overshadows the 'He.' Self-edification supplants the glorifying of God.[10]

Radical repentance does not seek to excuse or justify before God or man what the parish has done or failed to do. Mere self-improvement with moderate amounts of patchwork will not measure up to the demands of radical repentance. Polishing institutional brightwork to a high gloss will not get the parish auto with serious engine trouble running again. Stauffer's indictment calls into question presuppositions in many a parish and shakes to the very foundations all institutional pride and posturing. If any of this indictment is true for a parish, radical repentance is in order — a corporate repentance whereby the institutionalized parish is thrown on the rack until it goes through a kind of death where it will lose its life for the sake of Christ and the Gospel and be raised by the Spirit to receive the risen life in Christ from the heavenly Father.

Any of the following attitudes indicate the need for radical repentance. Pastors and prominent laymen versed in the Bible know what ought to be, but the imperative tends to fizzle into mere pious and wishful thinking. Pastors and prominent laymen in their devotion to the institutional parish may perhaps seek props to support the institution: alliance with the wealthy and influential or appeals to lesser motives such as sentiment or tradition. Some pastors and laymen are genuine in their devotion to the church but are too myopic or naive to understand how others are using them or what others are really doing with the parish. Others may be irked because their own prejudices have been touched: "You have no right to speak where I am sensitive."

As wrong as it is for the church to serve only itself, so is it wrong to abandon the chosen planting of God because it shows signs of self-adoration and blunted purpose. Conversely, we may be so overwhelmed and impressed by the call of God and the purpose of God in creating the church, that we blind ourselves to pious self-adoration and obvious will-to-power within the church. Pastors and loyal laymen should neither filter hard facts through rose-colored lenses nor should they pretend that reason for criticism does not exist.

Confusion Over Church's Mission

A root difficulty seems to be an overemphasis on the external structure, shape, and organizational details of the parish and a busy moving of administrative checkers without vital connection with the God-given purpose and mission service of the church.

Our confusion about the mission of the church comes to the surface almost any time we talk about missions. In the town and country parish there is precious little awareness that the local parish is God's cutting edge against the world, that "the end of the world" for anyone can be measured spiritually by the distance he is from Christ. Since the parish, in common thinking, is primarily an organization, missions must be some sort of extension of our organization: missions are what we *do* above and beyond what we *are* as a parish. Thus missions are pigeonholed to mean work far away or work among people less fortunate. Outreach to Indian Americans or migratory workers, work in the teeming tenements of the inner city or on a world-mission frontier may indeed be properly termed missions. During frontier days, when successive waves of scattered immigrants swept westward, then (so the thinking of some goes) rural parishes had a mission — but not in settled, successful, 20th-century America. Spike very rightly says: "There is no such thing as the stable, normal church — unchanged, uninfluenced by cultural shock and crisis — as over against less fortunate groups in American life who need mission work so they can be brought up to standard." [11] For example, few if any of the old solid Lutheran settlements such as St. Ansgar, Iowa, Frankenmuth, Mich., or Freistatt, Mo., remain as stable pockets of the Gospel's social and cultural penetration into society. The solemn and memorable words of John Donne (1573—1631) reecho their warning to mid-20th-century rural parishes: "Therefore never send to know for whom the bell tolls; it tolls for thee."

Faulty Image of Self and Rural Life

Instinctively many town and country people feel that the rural way of life is definitely superior to any form of urban living. If not quite God's ideal design for society, rural life is closer to a more natural pattern of living. Not only are they more satisfying, but rural work-patterns and institutions produce better people — folks that are more happy and hearty. Satisfaction with where and how they live they call living in "God's country."

Rural people like to view themselves as "just plain folks." They load this term to include living in a community of religious-minded people and among folks whose spoken word is as good as a written contract. Rural life preserves more wholesome family values; there are more intimate face-to-face relationships: "Everyone knows everybody; you can say hello to anyone."

Rural folk, however, need to be forcibly reminded that their notion of ideal community is faulty; there can be no easy identification of rural folkways with the church, the communion of saints. Many would readily admit this but then immediately express a nostalgic yearning for the old community friendliness in response to a death, birth, or wedding; to a house or barn raising; or to personal tragedy or loss of property. These former signs of close community have slipped badly, as nonfarm people commute to bigger towns and cities, as TV cuts into "visiting," and as the prosperous farmer spends more time on records and management decisions. A constant criticism is that people are too busy to "neighbor." However, such neighborliness is often little more than a reciprocal insurance and is usually confined only to the tight neighborhood or township in which you live, or it is directed to people with whom you get along socially. Pointedly excluded are the declassed "shack people," "who can't be trusted," or who "live like animals" — "they're bad." [12] Such identification is decidedly heretical. It is in opposition to the central doctrine that

God justifies sinners by grace through faith and for Jesus' sake. Such an attitude "tends to identify salvation with a particular social arrangement." The rural Christian errs fundamentally if he imagines that an "organic [rural] society and the existence of wholesome personal relationships" are what "make a man whole." The town and country parish must remind itself to "witness to the Christless [rural] man of an organic society that he is not whole unless he is organically linked with the living Christ in the community of faith which is the church." [13]

Town and country parishes need to see that radical repentance precludes any built-in advantage to any social structure. The living Word of the living Christ confronts all men alike with the same radical call to repentance and to wholehearted faith, total commitment, and loving, loyal service. Just as all distinctions of class, sex, and even religious and racial backgrounds faded for Christians of the first century, so today there must be no distinction between rural and urban and suburban (Gal. 3; Rom. 2). Rural Christians must see that a farmer loading grain is per se no closer to God than a warehouseman loading a semi; smalltown merchants are no more exempt from temptation to chisel on taxes than are suburban salesmen. Driving a mud-streaked late-model car down a gravel road rather than a shiny new one along a 6-lane freeway puts no one automatically closer to God. The large grain and feeder cattle operator maneuvering a new $9,000 combine may not even be as close to a Christian view of creation as the Negro lady who never sees a blade of grass in her slum area but lovingly tends three African violets in her cold-water flat.

Empire Building

Rural parishes are as guilty of empire building as are urban and suburban ones. Vidich and Bensman sketched the expansionist tendencies they found in Springdale when they noted that the job performances of pastors are judged by attendance and membership figures and the size of annual budgets. "In spite of the fact that total church membership is fairly constant, a church is viewed as not being dynamic unless it shows a continuous increase in these indices." [14] Empire building and overconcern with prestige loom in an ugly way when all six local pastors of a small village call on the new grade school principal but pay little or no attention to a hundred or more declassed or dechurched people. Empire building comes to the fore when in a town of 3,000 one church completes a building program that triggers 3 or 4 renovating or building programs. Empire building comes to the fore when a parish pays beady-eyed attention to St. Paul — the church across the street, not the apostle's letters and witness.

Intense Institutionalism

Buffeted by so many social shocks and economic shifts, many rural people may turtle-like defensively pull into their shell and resist any further change. In many rural areas, whether static or not, there is a deep pessimism and spreading despair in the face of seemingly irresistible social and economic-political shifts. They do not know which wave of sudden change or which application of the marketing revolution will hit them next. So little seems to be sure; nothing appears to have any deep roots. Widespread dread of factors not really understood or accounted for accentuates a withdrawal into the familiar and familial.

Though called to be the sphere where God's honor is to dwell, rural parishes under stress are sorely tempted to cling to the comfortably familiar. Unmindful that God's church is called into existence only by God's sovereign grace, in time of upheaval they may seek stability in the parish, an organization they can to some degree control or dominate. The church is theirs, not God's. Shanghai Smith, a profane Texas rancher, typifies this approach. Smith built a church on his ranch, and though he never went or belonged, he was intensely proud of the church he had erected for his ranch hands and their families. Someone once twitted him, "Shanghai, is it really true that you now belong to the church?" The snorted reply: "Hell no, the church still belongs to me."

Though 1-room school houses have long consolidated, creameries merged, and political units have grown toward greater interdependence, the town and country parish, especially the open country church, remains the object of waves of sentiment and is viewed as the lone brake providing some control on a way of life threatening to run away. In this view the body of Christ is the local organization to be controlled rather than an organism controlled by God. The New Testament speaks of the church living in God and growing in Him as a new people whose head and control center is the living Christ. Too often this high view of the church becomes so localized as to include only the familiar white frame building with the steep-pitched roof that Grandpa helped shingle 30 years ago and with the stained-glass window dedicated to Mama's sacred memory. The church becomes a place to which people are committed rather than a company of believers committed to the living Christ, His Word, and His mission.

Often people's loyalty is merely to the church building. Membership in rural areas is often not based on residence but on kinship. When people move to another area they tend to retain their membership in the former parish — often resisting transfer even though they have moved far from the effective parish area. Activity in the parish is certainly related to how close people live to the church building; a radius of 10—15 miles may be the outside limit for effective communication and participation. Further, many who are dechurched used to belong to parishes that have since disbanded. When the familiar ties to family unit, custom, or to a church building have been severed, the vacuum that is left has not been filled by loyalty to Christ. Rural people tend to identify the body of Christ with the familiar church in which they grew up.

This view of the church as place and building often turns on itself. When the security of the familiar building is threatened by a merger or consolidation, members will manipulate the organization to reach their own ends. A merger committee responded to the writer's question "What is better in the wider interest of God's church? Which procedure would be more within God's will?" by answering, "Don't ask us to answer those questions! We know what the only answer can be and we don't want to merge!" In a northern Minnesota parish of three congregations the largest congregation sent an invitation requesting a small struggling congregation six miles out in the open country to consider consolidation. The oblique answer came back in the form of a resolution to install stained glass windows costing several thousand dollars. In an area facing social change and shock, it may be very serious to blend loyalty to the church with the familiar institutional trimmings of the parish. Incidental trimmings such as the building and name of the church, the family pew, and the cemetery next to the church with Grandma's tombstone in it can become "the objects of supreme loyalty" and "our worship of them idolatry." [15]

Legalistic Morality

When judged by the Word of God, rural culture has apparently absolutized many of its customs and values as the will of God. The church in town and country too often succumbs to the temptation to trim God's will to what the rural community will tolerate and sanction. Sadly, much of this is motivated by a legalistic conformity which does not flow out of the inner tension and discipline of the Word of Christ. This legalism is reinforced by a view of Scripture as a code book.

Rural Christians so afflicted must all get over the provincial and prudish notion that their society is morally superior to other forms of society, and realize that moral purity comes not from physical separation from morally contaminated cities but alone from heart, mind, and will which dies with Christ daily and rises to His new life of grace. In looking down patronizingly upon urban and suburban life with its greater complexities, rural Christians tend to identify social environment with morality. Air pollution makes for polluted morals, while the purer rural air almost guarantees moral purity. As in the city, so in the small town, people crowd the bars of the VFW or club, slap each other on the back and talk heartily, but never really meet, say anything, or hear anything. As in the city so in the small town, doctors' offices are crowded by those sick of the pain of existence. As in the city, so in the small town, people cushion life with sedatives at night and stimulants in the morning. As in the city, so in the small town, people use one another in cheap love made possible by contraceptives, and when finished they toss away their partner as a disposable paper napkin and then wonder where fulfillment is. As in the city, so in the small town, there is an overweaning trust in the Big Machine, a confidence that inevitable advances are just around the corner.

Town and country Christians may rightly deplore high divorce rates, soaring illegitimate births, and lawlessness and crime of all descriptions. Certainly life in Christ is a life of order. Chaotic conditions are close when many sneeringly ignore and reject moral restraints.

However, the revolution in morals may mortally wound the negative morality whereby the average American congratulates himself on what he doesn't do. The Law never deals with trivialities; the Law doesn't congratulate a man for not having smoked filched cigarettes behind the barn when a boy. The Sermon on the Mount, contrary to American religion-in-general, does not sanction the national way of life but rips it to shreds. The sermon

67

is not the moral ideal for the Christless masses, but only for Christ's man, who by faith in Christ has received inner purity of heart and will to do God's will. Such a revolution in morals may help the town and country parish in its positive proclamation of the Good News that life in Christ is much more than edging nervously along a mortal tightrope; life in Christ is response to the inner tension and discipline of Christ's Word of judgment and mercy.

Overchurching

A typical village of 300 to 800 will often have 4 or 5 Protestant parishes competing from opposite corners of the main street. Let the area served by the writer serve as a negative example: the area center, a city of slightly more than 7,000 population, has 14 churches with 17 resident clergy; while the small village of 250 population, 17 miles to the south, has five competing churches with two resident clergy struggling to serve a constricting radius of 5 to 7 miles.

Town and country parishes must ask whether this is morally defensible. Inner-city slums may be so densely populated that 40 people will actually live in the basement coal bins of one tenement; many bins thus have more total population than the average square mile in the Great Plains. Is it morally defensible to set up struggling stations wherever there is a knot of people who favor the denomination and the color of the denomination's subsidy money? Ought not missions be established by priority of the greatest need? Doesn't the Gospel always reach out for those who are poor in spirit before going on to those who are rich? In the light of world mission needs in South America and East Asia, is it morally defensible to tie up so much pastoral manpower and congregational energy in competing rural programs? Dare the church in town and country make the Gospel convenient for a few without making it available to all?

Christians ought never minimize genuine confessional differ-

68

ences, nor should they discount division of church bodies along genuinely doctrinal grounds. However, Lutheran Christians in town and country ought to recognize that Article Seven of the Augsburg Confession makes agreement on the doctrine of the Gospel and the administration of the Sacraments "enough" for the true unity of the church. Far too often, perpetuation of strictly denominational programs has become necessary because parishes and church bodies had not resisted the temptation of self-preservation at all cost. Rather they have allowed social and economic conditions to mold them into "caste-organizations" rather than Christ-organisms — labels coined by H. Richard Niebuhr. Every effort to organizationally embody the church of Christ will represent a compromise with both the church and the world that can only be resolved by radical repentance and God's justifying grace. Too often, that inevitable compromise is welcomed rather than resisted "to the blood." Pride in such easy compromises Niebuhr denounces as "unacknowledged hypocrisy" and resounding defeat for the Gospel of God.[16]

Overchurching causes pastors of multiple parishes to leapfrog all over the landscape. Much like the milk haulers from various competing creameries, three or more pastors will many times travel the same stretch of highway, barely waving at one another as they pass each other at 70 miles per hour to reach the second or third Sunday service on time.

Selective Involvement

While protesting that they are involved with Christ and His church, town and country parishes often mean by that involvement with their own cozy church group and to a lesser extent with their own church body through its world mission program. Involvement with the mass of humanity is neatly excised.

One of the sad side-effects of overchurching and intense competition between churches in small towns is that each tends to lose awareness of responsibility to the total community. This danger is accentuated when parishes are small, inbred or struggling; their energies are dissipated in the struggle to keep their own program and pattern going. Surveys of rural population have shown that those not directly engaged in agriculture, the growing two thirds of the rural population, are at least half unchurched.

Few town and country parishes have organized a systematic outreach to the unchurched. Energetic, mission-minded pastors often stumble across homes and entire areas where no pastor has visited in 25 years or more. In a 3-year study of "Springdale," New York, Vidich and Bensman discovered that 1,300 out of 1,700 total population did not go to church, nor were they the object of any mission work. Some had been approached by one or more pastors, had consistently resisted, and so were written off. A second group were those who were written off out of hand as not being church material: "the immoral, the irresponsible, those without self-respect." Few if any church people were more aware of them than of a cigarette butt or a garbage can. Pastors and concerned laymen "either do not see the unchurched or they have no desire to pollute the church membership with socially undesirable types. This attitude results in an almost total neglect of local missionary opportunities." [17]

A prerequisite for church membership in many town and country parishes is that those to be evangelized must first "think as we think, farm as we farm, talk as we talk, and dress as we dress." The notion that rural nonfarm residents, factory workers, and shack people living in rural slums are "just not our kind" stands in almost direct contrast to the indecent scramble to ring the doorbells of new hospital staff, school teachers, or others whose social and economic position might enhance the prestige of the parish successful in landing them as members.

Town and country parishes and their leaders must take seriously the Gospel's insistence that we love people as they are and that our neighbor is anyone who at that point of time is spiritually, emotionally, mentally or physically poorer than we ourselves. Town and country leaders must ask how can the inconsistent attitude of selective involvement be squared with the traditionally generous [?] support of world missions? Do rural Christians love people only at long distance?

WHAT MUST BE BORN IN TOWN AND COUNTRY PARISHES

Genuine Repentance and Forgiveness

Small-town American Christians need to say and mean the words of the common confession. They need to experience the relief of knowing that they are God's sinning but forgiven children as they turn heart and life to Christ. They need to know that the town and country church of God can be radically purged and made clean by the Word of the living Christ.

There would be much inward peace if pastors and laymen alike would admit that they have permitted the body of Christ to become ossified into a self-serving institution. The Roman Church was certainly responsible for the Inquisition and the extreme measures of Counter-Reformation scheming that prompted the bloody St. Bartholomew's Night massacre. However, the men who planned and guided were convinced that these extremes were needed to preserve the institution of the church, God's chosen vehicle to bear His Word. Hence, any heretics threatening the stability of the bearer of the Word should be liquidated before institution and Word are destroyed. Like other institutions the parish is not exempt from the characteristic danger that it become an end in itself, tending to justify and conserve its own existence rather than to propagate the Gospel at the expense of expending itself.

Real relief of conscience and mind would come if town and

71

country Christians would openly admit that rural areas are in a period of difficult transition and admit that as parishes they have failed to face these changes. Rural failure is characteristically masked behind a conspiracy of silence. The "etiquette of gossip" dictates that negative statements be made only in intimate groups of two or three, but not publicly, for that would disturb surface appearances of success, harmony, and tranquillity. Where public forthrightness is lacking, the deceptive outward image of success goes unchallenged and uncorrected.

Many small-town Christians would be greatly relieved to confess how inconsistent and two-faced they have been. The face the average small-town man shows to the world is that of the "hardworking, God-fearing, unsophisticated person" while simultaneously "responding to the glamorous invitations of the mass world." While driving cars "designed for continental playboys," and dressing in the latest New York fashions, he feels "secretly corrupted but ashamed to be anything but hearty and just plain folks." [18] Rural folk also feel the tremendous pull of life purposes patterned around the "success system," with its constellation of related goals: success, prestige, money, power, and security. Small-town and rural goals are often very little different from urban. Rural folk should admit that a growing number are outer-directed, seeking their stance and pattern of life decisions from those around them. They should admit that, although there are still many inner-directed and pioneering types in town and country, neither of Riesman's patterns (p. 62, n. 9) conforms to the will of God: "Don't let the world around you squeeze you into its own mould" (Rom. 12:1 Phillips). It would be wholesome to admit and confess that the rural virtues of hard work, thrift, and personal achievement, accompanied by a deep sense of vocation and pride in the personal touch of craftsmanship — although deeply longed for — have to a large extent been eroded by the acids of modern technology.

72

Resources for Renewal — Discipleship

Unsure of itself, bewildered and confused about its mission, the town and country parish dazedly begins to pick its way through the rubble of a formerly stable and settled social and economic structure. Even such unsettled conditions are no real disadvantage for the parish that is ready to meet the living Lord and follow Him. By His gift of grace the risen Christ presses home His sovereign claims on the confused town and country parish, summoning it into discipleship. In the midst of deep turmoil and confusion, the Lord Jesus calls people to follow Him in discipleship. Peter and Andrew went down to the lake to fish but actually they had gone to meet Jesus — He had decided that (Mark 1:16-20). Matthew went down to the tax office only to be faced with the startling claim, "Follow Me" (Matt. 9:9). Jesus had come to town. The woman of Samaria who had had five husbands and was living with another man in a common-law relationship ostensibly went to the well to get water for her household needs. But she found Jesus — or rather, Jesus found her (John 4). Paul on the Damascus road was reviewing his strategy to wipe out the disturbing influence of that jailbird Jesus and His ragtag followers, when the risen Christ confronted and subdued him. (Acts 9)

It is overwhelmingly significant that Jesus calls men to Himself: "Follow Me." He Himself is the content of His call; the entire center of gravity is found in Jesus. The bare command, the grace-filled invitation comes: "Follow Me," and men are expected to drop all and obey. Jesus extends to them nothing but the best and most beneficial, offering as answer to their unspoken, unformed cries: "Come to *Me* all who labor and are heavy laden, and *I* will give you rest" (Matt. 11:28). In calling Christians to Himself, our Lord expects those who follow to draw their life from Him in loving faith, faithful love, and loyal mission service. They are to abide in the Vine and as the branches, the extended

73

growing edge of the Vine, they are to bear more and more fruit in the world. (John 15:3-5)

Jesus calls His followers to Himself: "Take up your cross and walk in My footsteps." He calls them away from other things: the consuming chase after money in daily occupations like fishing and banking (Peter, Andrew, and Matthew), or from running after sex or prestige to fill an empty life. As God's pilgrim people, followers of Jesus are not to settle down comfortably into the values others place on life. Those looking for the heavenly rest (Heb. 4 and 12) will accumulate less baggage, be weighed down with less anxieties, and be more ready to cope with the sudden shifts and unexpected situations into which the Lord calls them.

The Aramaic meaning of "the word 'cross' meant something sticking out of the ground," most "generally . . . a tent peg." The Bedouin sheikh ordering a move tells the women of his harem, "Take up the cross [tent peg] and follow me." D. T. Niles expands the meaning of Jesus' cryptic statement: "You cannot follow me by staying where you are. You must break camp. You think that your security lies in the well-trodden paths of yesterday. I tell you it lies only in following Me along the unknown paths of tomorrow and sharing there both my passion and my victory." [19]

"Anyone who wishes to be a follower of Mine must leave self behind; he must take up his cross, and come with Me. Whoever cares for his safety is lost; but if a man will let himself be lost for My sake and for the Gospel, that man is safe." (Mark 8:34-36 NEB)

The Parish — Yeast of Renewal

Many a rural parish in mid-20th-century America has an inner yearning for a deep commitment that will ring true even with upsetting facts and trends staring it in the face. Above all, many a rural parish needs to fasten its trust and loyalty on Him who will take it far beyond its depth but give it rootage, purpose, and permanence in the bargain.

The sociologist may be very aware of cultural factors, the inertia and resistance to change that makes the parish in town and country seemingly impervious to becoming what it really should be. To him the town and country parish cannot be the local ship of the church until this or that symptom of barnacled institutionalism can be scraped off or until the gaping holes and leaks are repaired. Much sociological effort is directed to these points. Pastors and laymen may also feel that only after extensive and successful repairs will the Gospel take hold. Luther in the Smalcald Articles indicated that the essence of the church was so transparently obvious that even a 7-year-old could know that it consisted of the lambs who hear the voice of their Shepherd. The Good News is the only message that is completely and absolutely good; God loves men and calls them into unity with Him in His risen newness of life, into the community of believers, the church. Since the church is gathered around the Word of Christ and the Sacraments and proclaims, hears, obeys, acts on the Good News, anyone who looks upon the church may truly look on Christ.

The renewal Christ offers to the world of mankind and to the world of town and country is a hidden, inner one, because the Gospel is hidden and innerly active. The mission that Christ has given His church is not primarily that of changing conditions and institutions of society by frontal attack. Rather the parish is to act like yeast that raises the entire measure of pasty dough. While never really becoming identical with it, the yeast thoroughly permeates the lump, transforming it into a bulging, heaving mass of bubbling energy. The yeast does not wait for the dough to begin to rise before it lets loose its powers of expansive force. The parish, like yeast, is called to let the powerful reign of God's love in Christ move with compelling force in its own midst and thus serve as a force that leavens the entire lump of town and country society.

Dedicated Pastors [20]

Georges Bernanos depicts the loving ministry of a young priest coming to his first parish:

> Just three months today since my appointment to this Parish of Ambricourt. Already three months. . . . This morning I prayed hard for my parish, my poor parish, my first and perhaps my last, since I ask no better than to die here. My parish! The words can't even be spoken without a kind of soaring love. . . . But as yet the idea behind them is so confused. I know that my parish is a reality, that we belong to each other for all eternity: it is not a mere administrative fiction, but a living cell in the everlasting church. But if only the good God would open my eyes and unseal my ears, so that I might behold the face of my parish! The look in the eyes . . . these would be the eyes of all Christianity, of all parishes — perhaps of the poor human race itself. Our Lord saw them from the cross. . . .[21]

"Our Lord saw them from the cross. . . ." Most pastors coming directly from the seminary to the town and country parish have middle-class backgrounds, and come from urban or suburban areas. This is no built-in handicap if the pastor shows that he is bound to his parish's life with ties that cannot be broken. By his entire public and private attitude he must show that without pretense he loves his parish for Christ's sake. Every pastor needs a personal vision and experience of the grace of Christ, and a vision of the world inside and outside the parish transformed after being joined to Christ. Such a view is both salutary and utopian: the pastor loves them as they are and as they may yet be under the Spirit's blessing. Such a view is the Spirit's gift as a consequence flowing from genuine conversion. The town and country pastor may have an advantage in seeing his people as the Lord saw them from the cross. The pastor serving a small community is often in a better position than his urban counterpart to counsel a couple with marriage difficulties, a troubled teen-ager, someone in need of vocational help, or a bereaved family. Person-to-person contact with sheriff, surgeon, psychologist, and educator about parishioners is easily made.

". . . If only the good God would open my eyes and unseal my ears, so that I might behold the face of my parish!" As a realist obsessed by facts, the town and country pastor will have a torrent of eager questions about rural life, farming techniques, and conservation practices. By rolling up his sleeves and pitching in, the pastor will discover for himself the nature of farm or factory work; he will see firsthand how drudgery affects vocation and motivations; he will gain better insight into how firmly the pastor is shut from their thought and work world. The town and country pastor by his whole attitude will avoid pretense and yawning half-interest. Rather patiently seeking exact information, he should be ready to revise his point of view in the light of new insights. Through consultation with the county agent and Soil Conservation and Stabilization personnel he will learn how best to approach rural people. Early in his ministry he will get to know the sheriff, the police chief, the town council, school administrators, and other public officials. He will secure reports of local and regional planning groups. Since Christ is "subsistent truth" (Abbé Michonneau's phrase), he will seek and gain facts to get a clear look at the face of his parish.

He should be an uneasy man, concerned and moved by people's rejection of the church. Always easily shocked, not at what people think of him, but at what people think of his Lord, the pastor should be willing to accept the cold hostility and defensiveness of a parish that has seen pastors come and go for years. No amount of chilliness, inertia, or unpleasantness should blunt his Christlike compassion for men or leave him blasé. By paying the price of identifying himself with the community and its problems and by understanding the defensiveness of a small town parish, the rural pastor should be ready to accept and outlast both.

Jesus' call to take up the cross and follow Him means that the

77

rural pastor should be willing to be a victim without whining or self-pity. He himself is expendable as the reign of Christ within his parish moves on, even, if necessary over the pastor's own body. No rural parish, however backward or deprived of confident leadership in the past, should be thought of as anything less than first-rate. If the pastor is to effectively proclaim the Gospel of a God who by definition is Love, the pastor must first love the people of the parish in God's name, individually and unselfishly. He should love his parish enough to stay for an enduring ministry, not hopping like a grasshopper from parish to parish, seeking advances. Rural parishes also live by the law of self-preservation and after experiencing years of short ministries and long vacancies, are likely to suspiciously withhold themselves. Neither parish nor community will expect the pastor to stay as a permanent resident; often within a small village there is a complete turnover of pastors every 5 to 10 years. Rural parishes are not for those who consider them a good place to study and then move up to "bigger and better things," nor for those who have not made the grade elsewhere. How can parishes be expected to face social upheaval if the present rapid movement of the clergy out of troubled areas is not halted?

The rural pastor needs both a vision of his whole parish and a vision of the whole church. Unless the pastor seriously attempts to understand the different social segments of the typical town and country parish, he may be most attracted to those with a background similar to his own, the business men and prosperous farmers. To be effective he need not completely approve, but he should understand and if possible appreciate the minds of the traditional farmer and the factory worker and the grinding poverty of rural slum dwellers. Otherwise, in his pride in personal values and standards he also may overlook those by and large ignored in the past. Also he should have a vision of God's grand plan for the universe coming true in Christ, and of every person in the parish enlisted in the church's mission. He ought not be dragged into the minimum of what the parish expects of its pastor: preaching on Sundays, teaching confirmation class, visiting in the parish only because it is expected and traditional, and getting and keeping the societies' wheels rolling. Rather he should use every meeting and every organization to teach a glowing vision of the entire church coming true within the rural parish. Through planned pastoral visits he should sit down by appointment for at least an hour with each family every year; through profiles, questionnaires, and Bible study guides he should relate life in Christ to daily decisions and life patterns and undergird the church's mission as expressed in parish and family life.

The town and country pastor is extremely visible in the life of a rural community. In this sort of goldfish bowl existence he and his family can expect to be very closely watched. Leaders of rural parishes will often attempt to trim their pastors' views to their own customs and likings. While most farmers see value in cross-breeding pigs and invariably plant hybrid corn, they often see little value in hybridizing parish thought. However, the pastor should resist the temptation to go along with what community and parish expect of him: to be a good fellow, one who is non-controversial and who won't rock settled community patterns.

Through constant study of Bible and theology he should counteract the widespread suspicion that an intellectual cannot be a good pastor; by serving them the Bread and Water of life he truly serves his congregation.

Mission and Parish Strategy

Too often the understanding of mission in town and country has been too narrow; "the world is my parish" has been subverted into "the parish is my world." A radical shift in definition is needed.

What actually matters in the practice of mission is "to be," not "to act." Because the parish has forgotten what God wants it to be, it does not know how to act. To act without thinking about what it means to be degenerates into a minor rearrangement of parish structure, a reshuffling of old concerns, another centering on community, family, and building. Precisely this concern for self-perpetuation by propping up organizations and by padding familiar customs in the name of Christ has so compromised the parish that even the majority of its members no longer take its claims seriously. Where there is little sense of being God's pilgrim people on the march, even the food for the march, Word and Sacrament, taste stale and dull under the white spire. Where there is little sense of being the extension of Christ into the world as His body, living His risen life and continuing in the world His ministry of reconciliation incarnate, Christ's revolutionary ethic of love undergoes a transmutation into something inoffensive, sensible, and commonplace. The demands of following Christ no longer shock with their urgency — nor do they give meaning and structure to life. No longer knowing what it is and hence not knowing how to act, the parish too often marks time, going through familiar pious motions.

Dr. John Heuss, rector of historic Trinity Parish at the foot of New York City's Wall Street, suggests in a sermon on "The True Function of a Christian Church" that every parish needs some thoughtful group of men and women charged with ongoing responsibility for asking three basic questions and finding their answers:

1. What is [the mission of the church and] the true religious job of this parish?

2. How can all that is done in this whole parish set forward that true religious task?

3. To what extent is everything . . . we are doing changing the lives of the people involved? [22]

Too seldom are such fundamental questions ever asked. Far less frequently are the questions honestly confronted or given satisfactory answers, for they call into question so much that is traditionally "religious." Everyone assumes that this is what the pastor is trained for and paid to do. Listen to the verdict of a 4-year study of a typical county in Mid-America: ". . . very few church or nonchurch people have seemingly given much thought to these questions. Apparently religion in its social manifestation and in the organized life of churches simply *is,* and it is the function of the churches to foster this." [23] Thorough Every Member Visits for stewardship or Spiritual Life Missions may be steps in the right direction, but they too can degenerate into sewing patches on organizational weakness.

Self-study, a systematic way of finding, interpreting, and acting on facts gathered by a thoughtful group in the parish, is one hopeful pattern being followed by many church bodies as they struggle toward rediscovery of the mission of the church in town and country areas.[24] Self-studies are guided by sociologically-aware pastors and laymen with a vision of the Kingdom and a Biblical understanding of the church's mission. Any concerned parent who knows how to read the thermometer can see his child has a 104° fever; but only the physician's diagnosis will reveal whether tonsilitis, measles, or pneumonia is the cause of the fever.

Self-study can never be anything but a painful process as parishes begin to operate on the basis of facts rather than sentiment and tradition inherited from the horse-and-buggy days. Such reappraisal will be but a mechanical following of a precut pattern developed on some church planner's drawing board unless parishes look at themselves through the radical concepts of death and rebirth and are aware of the need for repentance and the risen life under grace.

Deep preliminary resistance may go even deeper when Christ's will for the parish is spelled out in radical terms of death and rebirth. Some led by the Spirit will believe, learn, and break through their shells of organizational self-preservation. Others may cling all the more tenaciously to the traditional when confronted with the shock of change. Such Biblical searching and self-study will always show that the shape of the parish's mission and strategy is predetermined by Jesus' death and resurrection. We come to God through Him who died for all on a cross; mission may lead to the sacrifice and death of the present parish so that others might have access to God. Paul explicitly tied his ministry to a close identification with Jesus' death:

> For continually, while still alive, we are being surrendered into the hands of death, for Jesus' sake, so that the life of Jesus also may be revealed in this mortal body of ours. Thus death is at work in us and life in you. (2 Cor. 4:11, 12 NEB. See also Col. 1:24.)

The grace of God was costly, costing God His Son and the deep degradation of His identification with mankind: a drafty barn, a criminal's cross, and a borrowed grave that we might know His rich grace (2 Cor. 8:8). Is the parish with a servant's mission greater than its Servant-Lord (Matt. 10:23)? He wants the parish to enter life fully and as leaven to run the risk of mixing itself into all the dough of the world; no longer can it live in its safe, familiar patterns (Luke 13:21). As salt the parish must be rubbed into the meat of life to keep it from spoiling; it must be thrown into the soup to impart a good flavor (Matt. 5:13). As seed, the parish must expect to be taken by its Lord and scattered into the most unfamiliar places, among most unsavory people not of its kind or class — there to grow among the tares until the harvest of the Last Day. (Matt. 13:24-30; 36-43)

Such a concept of mission would involve the strategic discovery that all forms of parish life and expression exist not for their own sake but for the sake of Jesus and the Gospel. The parish must guard against Satan's evil work of warping and twisting the church's vision and values so that the parish safeguards them for their own importance. While the church is historically conditioned and does not start out from scratch, many traditionally important

82

things, if need be, could be discarded as excess baggage for a church on an expedition. Traditional means of administration could go — synods, districts, conferences, church councils, and voters' assemblies; traditional modes of mission could go — seminaries and training schools; radio, TV, and literature missions; and organized evangelistic efforts; the traditional prestige of church bodies could go — influence in newspapers and TV, hearings given the church's scholars and spokesmen, the impressive role of the influential who belong. All of these conceivably could go, and the church would still be the church if it retained Word and Sacraments and made some provision for a teaching and proclaiming ministry. In and behind some of the present forms and methods the Evil One busily works on our self-deceit, as when he suggests that church body and parish forget their Lord and mission and remember their own importance and image: "Fall down and worship me and all the kingdoms of the world will be yours as well." (Matt. 4:8, 9)

Small Groups — The Remnant

Carl E. Braaten, professor of systematic theology at the Maywood Lutheran seminary, says that if he were a pastor again he would work toward awareness of mission through small groups.

> I believe now that were I to be pastor again, I would honeycomb the parish with small cells, study groups, meeting once a week. I would spend my time teaching them to be the church, to do what I was spending my time doing in the neighborhood, something they could actually do much more effectively. They would be taught what it means to be a believer in Jesus Christ and a member of His church today. We would discuss how this works itself out in the actual lives of our members. . . . I would rather now work as the communists, indeed as the first Christians did. I would think my first obligation is to minister to those who are already Christians, so that they might become a community, a ministering community in the world.[25]

Our Lord worked with small groups, molding the Twelve for three years as the center of a reconstituted people of God. Small study groups deliberately work with the principles of discipleship and the Old Testament remnant within the nation. God's Spirit works not only comprehensively, but also selectively. While God intends to work universally, He uses a limited method and instrument — men whom He calls to Himself. Also with respect to workers "Many are called, but few are chosen" (Matt. 22:14). The church is for the world; yet as branch of the Vine of God it needs to be pruned (John 15:2); the confessing people of God will necessarily be a reduced remnant.

Basically a study group seeks to develop and expand a core of committed, deeply dedicated leadership at the heart of the parish. Three things form the center: prayer, intense Bible study, and witness as the external expression of this Spirited fellowship — all in relation to the world. All respond to Scripture; no one-way flow of Biblical insight or monologues delivered by the leader should dominate the study group. Compelled by the Word to pray for one another, for the world inside and outside the parish, the group is better equipped to serve as the cutting edge of witness to fellow members and to the world around the parish. There is of course danger that these small study groups become institutionalized, with an exclusive holier-than-thou attitude that makes those outside the group uneasy and drives others away. Subjective preoccupation with personal religious experience may anesthetize rather than stimulate witness and mission-service. No random application of small groups will fill past vacuums but rather Spirited activity following hard upon repentant, Bible-filled, prayerful waiting for a new descent of the Holy Spirit.

Basic to successful expression of study groups are three factors: (1) A personal experience of God's grace in Jesus Christ by those who participate, whereby faith is not merely a religious concept, but a "personal possession." (2) Such a committed remnant will find itself involved in conflict and tension as it works for "upheaval and revolution within the conventional frame-

84

work" of the rural parish. Labor pains precede any birth; where yeast permeates, things do not go quietly but with expansive force. (3) Such a remnant should be drawn from different backgrounds and levels of parish life as together people "explore [the joys and] demands of Christian discipleship." [26]

In static or declining communities sometimes declining vigor of aging membership, sameness of outlook, or the threat of censure by relatives may cut short the ability to cross-fertilize points of view. Dr. Shirley Greene's case studies of 12 congregations underscore the role of traditional leaders in meeting challenges of ferment on the urban fringe: "In general, our conclusion was that a basic clue to the degree of success achieved by these particular churches lay in the presence of a substantial group of old-timers who were quite clear as to the true nature of the church and the focus of their ultimate loyalty." [27] Disheartened pastors ought not automatically assume that traditional leaders will oppose any change; nor should they delude themselves into thinking that any innovation is better than the old way.

Comprehensive Involvement

All surveys this writer has studied spotlight a glaring tendency for town and country parishes to come into existence, to be, and to remain one-class churches. "Birds of a feather flock together"; the feathers of the parish "bird" may be national origin, language, occupation, family ties, social standing, or prestige. The call of our Lord "Follow Me" indicates that He is already outside of the artificial walls many have built. In going beyond the dullness of one-stratum sameness, parishes must get comprehensively involved and stop getting their cues for outreach from self-serving questions like, "Where are the people who will best fit in, or are most like us?" and "Who is easier to reach?" Perhaps the decline in church vocations might be due in part to youth's sensing the inconsistency of pastors being caretakers for a select, chosen group.

Many town and country people in settled communities do not understand the values and the mental set of the blue-collar worker, the industrial technician who commutes to the neighboring town. Their working and shopping in the larger town, the different style in which they live, their interest in car models, furniture, rugs, and color combinations in the home leave them socially isolated. On the other side, the job-centered factory worker usually finds exciting fellowship with his fellow workers, bowling league, or hunting and fishing pals. Much of the parish's program to him seems rather dull and bloodless. Since the parish life he sees is comfortably settled in a pattern he is not interested in, and since it seems that they are not interested in him, he instinctively senses that the life of the parish is merely another type of secular culture. He reasons: "Why belong to another organization when I already bowl two nights a week and watch the fights and ball games on the weekend?" In one 4-year survey of a typical Corn Belt county, the blue-collar group was underrepresented in all Protestant churches in the county; while the total membership of all Roman parishes, with one exception, reflected faithfully the proportion of blue-collar workers living in their parish area.[28]

Even easier to ignore are the rural slums and their poverty-stricken inhabitants. Step into a rural slum home. This one is a three-room shack. Against one wall is a junk-littered dresser; a dilapidated daybed and tattered armchair fill out the furnishings of the "parlor." In two beds and the daybed seven people sleep. No plumbing and no electricity; two kerosene lamps provide a yellow, smoky light. Water is carried in by buckets. An ancient, iron woodburning stove heats the house and cooks the food. Broken windows are covered by cardboard winter and summer. In hot weather flies are everywhere. Rural slum dwellers may be found in economically depressed areas in all regions of the United States.

Pastors and laymen may be tempted to set the parish house

in order to get better prepared for evangelism. Self-evident though it seems, it is in some respects a mistake. The only real prerequisite for evangelism is the preaching of the Gospel. Where the Gospel has been proclaimed, the only further way to ready a parish for evangelism is by the work of evangelism. The mission of the Savior to this earth makes missionaries; the Evangel makes evangelists. Thorough canvasses and systematic once-a-month training, equipping and sending out of callers, steady contact with prospects through letters, tracts and newsletters, and other steps are sensible evangelistic administration. Yet parishes need not go to heroic lengths to prepare for evangelism, which naturally flows from the Evangel.

Town and country parishes may believe themselves to be friendly but fail to leave that impression on outsiders. Sometimes the parish is preoccupied or ingrown. Members feel at home because they belong to the little circle of intimates with membership for years, even generations, essentially composed of similar members of the same families. Customs of long standing having the appearance of being "universal, perennial, and even sacred, may seem strange and meaningless" to outsiders.[29] Town and country parishes faced with influx of membership should be flexible enough to revise cherished customs and practices if necessary, out of love acknowledging, "Their ways are not our ways."

Coordinated Planning

Basic to evangelistic outreach and mission-service is the conviction that people and not ethnic, clan, or geographic boundaries, make up the parish. This runs counter to the nonterritorial principle now in force in most Protestant parishes. Parishes of the Church of Rome have traditionally avoided duplication and overlapping of effort and have succeeded in covering most areas under the blanket of assigned parish responsibility. Whether or not the responsibility assigned by the bishop is also felt is up for discussion. But the Church of Rome in town and country has a vast advantage in knowing who is responsible for what.

Professor Glenn I. Nelson, a rural sociologist at the University of Minnesota, in a yet unpublished study of Meeker County, Minn., describes one of the dangers inherent in nonterritorial parishes. Some areas are overlooked and not served:

Stereotyped Areas

In areas where a high proportion of the church members belong to one church body, the area is stereotyped as being entirely composed of members of that church body. As a consequence, residents of that area who may not prefer the dominant church body often are not serviced by any religious organization.

The reality of this situation is supported by three findings of this study relative to one area of the county. The northern portion of the county has the highest proportion of persons belonging to the Roman Catholic Church. As a consequence the northern part of the county is stereotyped as being an "all-Catholic" area. However, in actual fact less than half of the residents of the civil divisions investigated, with the exception of two areas, belong to this church body.

Secondly, this area is systematically considered to be outside the area of responsibility of the pastors of many of the Protestant groups in the county (Figure 5).

Finally, conversations with county residents concerning the religious organization elicited, spontaneously, a stereotype of the area as being composed entirely of members of one church body.

As a consequence of these and perhaps other factors one finds the greatest proportion of unchurched individuals are located in this area of the county.[30]

Spotting parish memberships on uniform maps would reveal pockets of unchurched due to stereotyping or some other reason. If, for example, all Lutheran parishes in a county could be induced to work coordinately on such a mapping project, each would benefit by seeing more clearly where it is in relation to its area of responsibility. In Clark County, Wis., local congregations of the ALC, LCA, and Missouri Synod worked coordinately, if not cooperatively, in such a mapping effort.

If people make the church, possibly a minimum of 1,000—1,500 could be set as the norm for parishes — with the minimum in Great Plains states somewhat lower because of lower density of population. Such a concept would demand far greater coordination between church bodies than heretofore. Even if church bodies for confessional reasons could not cooperate in every respect, coordinated efforts are desperately needed to correct overchurching and wasteful use of manpower. Acceptance of the concept that people form parish boundaries would demand drastic overhaul and realignment of parishes, would add new churches in some places, and would close them in others. But such a concept would be a way of dealing with population shifts in declining rural areas and of meeting sudden influxes of new residents on the urban fringe. Such a flexible concept would mean commitment to *the* church in town and country but not necessarily commitment to any specific parish in town and country.

Such coordinated planning should not be too high a hurdle since most parishes in town and country already cooperate in less important areas of "externals." Congregations reserve traditional dates for Christmas programs "so the people from Grace Church can come too." Whichever church sponsors the pancake supper or ice cream social makes sure first that no other parish is having a ham and chicken dinner at the same time. The parish, a pilgrim society, should be mobile enough to meet such shifts. District mission boards could assist parishes at a crossroad in their life by providing self-study services for congregations in transition.

Equipping the Saints

Dr. Victor Obenhaus, professor at Chicago Theological Seminary, interprets vital Christian faith in a typical county of Mid-America, with information gained through a 4-year, 2-phase set of interviews. Approximately 1,200 people were interviewed in Corn County, the pseudonym given the Corn Belt county. The

evidence gathered in Corn County indicates that Biblical understanding is low in all denominations represented. Main Town,
the county seat, has the advantages of a concentration of government offices, banking services, schools, and farm organizations.
Despite these advantages in Main Town, only 60% of the Protestants and only one third of the Roman Catholics could designate
a difference between the Old and New Testaments. If parishioners
do not know Jesus' story of the Good Samaritan, chances are
they will be even less informed about other New Testament
teaching. Less than one third of those interviewed could translate the story of the Good Samaritan into "an admonition to
provide aid for others." More than one third of the Methodists,
United Lutherans, and Congregationalists interviewed had no idea
of any meaning to the story. This should prompt pastors of
church bodies observing the church year, who read the story
every 13th Sunday after Trinity, to tear their hair in dismay.[31]

The need is for family-centered education and Biblical teaching.
No longer can pastors and laymen assume that town and country
Christians pray, even at meals, or that they regularly conduct
family devotions. The pastor would do well to follow the pattern
of the Lord Jesus. He preached to the thronging crowds, but
above all He taught in personal and intimate groups. After
preaching He often took the disciples aside, answering questions
and giving insight into the heavenly Father's mind and heart.
Jesus first taught, then sent the disciples teaching (Matt. 10).
Pastors would do well to teach "from house to house," blanketing
the parish's homes with Bible study and question-answer sessions
designed to teach and equip how to read the Bible and how to
pray or conduct family worship. Pastors should "equip God's
people for work in His service, to the building up of the body
of Christ" (Eph. 4:12 NEB). The Every-Member-Visit pattern
is a modern application of Biblical teaching, well suited to town
and country adaptation.

The town and country pastor should ask whether he has left teaching to well-intentioned but poorly qualified laymen or women. The pastor should consider whether he should not direct all parish education rather than leave it in the hands of whoever is willing and has the time. As director of education the pastor could seriously examine, if practiced, indiscriminate baptizing without provision for spiritual growth in the home. Placing water on the infant's head in the name of the Triune God marks that child with the cross and the command to "Follow" for the rest of his life. However, children are sometimes baptized in rural parishes when the pastor feels the pressure of family solidarity in the shadow of an uncle who was an elder and contributes well. House plants get better care than baptized children in some instances. House plants at least have conditions for growth; they are not placed into a snow bank in zero weather and expected to do anything but shrivel.

The rural parish has a great task of education if it is going to train its youth to see the church as more than the familiar white-frame building back home; youth must be trained to transfer and adapt to parishes in larger towns and cities. The town and country parish ministers to a passing parade; when youth get their high school diploma in one hand, they pick up their suitcase with the other and head for the city. Town and country parishes should see this as a great challenge not as a source of depression. It's a Biblical principle for parishes as well as pastors that you know you won't reap everything you sow (1 Cor. 3:5-9). The "sending church" concept would be more vivid if the ladies' aid would write those who have transferred within the last 10 years, ask them to describe the parishes and positions of leadership they now hold, and then read excerpts from the responses during services or insert them in the parish newsletter. The sending of well-prepared youth would be an asset for the rural parish, which gains perspective and encouragement by being "better if not bigger."

The growing number of retired and elderly people in small-town America must somehow be better served by the parish. Retired farmers and formerly active businessmen could be recruited for small study groups and for active witness to the parish and community. Such recruitment will not only fill up empty hours but will aid them in building up others in that faith by which they themselves continue to live and die.

With the increased amount of leisure because of the decline from 70 to 40 hours in the workweek, much of life for those outside of agriculture is measured by how leisure time is spent rather than by how the living is made. Parishes in the resort areas of the country, such as the Mid-South and the timberland areas such as Minnesota, Wisconsin, and Michigan, could train and recruit for positive witness members who are resort owners; cabins could be provided Bibles and Gospel-centered literature and tracts. Possibly young people who serve as waitresses or guides should be trained by pastors and resort owners for witness of life and lip to vacationers.

Both of these suggestions stress the Christian's calling as comprising all the daily tasks and opportunities God gives along with the forgiveness of sins; both cut across the popular notion of separate but scarcely equal secular and sacred spheres. When Luther rediscovered the Christian's calling there was wide agreement as to social roles in that stable society. In mid-20th century not only has the rate of change spurted furiously, but relationships are much more complex; they are no longer face-to-face. No longer can the sanctified common sense of the Christian be counted on to provide ethical direction in many areas.

The farmer needs to be warned of arrogance, a danger of big-machine farming. Technology's easy triumphs may prompt the farmer toward assuming a big-man — little-god attitude. Heavy investment in machinery and plant expansion may be accompanied by a greed for quick profits and irreverent use of soil. The rural factory worker feels disconnected from his job. Tiring less quickly then men, machines often require three men working in shifts to keep up with them. In shift work the person, not the machine, becomes the interchangeable unit. Pay by the hour further depersonalizes work by centering on the job to be done and not on the person who does the job. Both mechanized agriculture and industry, though amoral in and of themselves, tend to be used in such a way that God is rejected or left out of the work picture; the church's assertion that the life and work of man take on meaning only in relation to God is denied. Thus the worker becomes just another productive unit among the total number of productive objects — animate or mechanized.

Vocational fellowships, on the European scene for over 30 years, could equip Christians to confront an environment that takes it for granted that God is irrelevant. Dean Louis Almen notes many advantages to such vocational fellowships and work conferences: Just the "very existence of such a group witnesses to the fact that the Christian faith is meant to embrace the world." Other advantages are group problem-solving, seeing problems of vocation from the uniquely personal vantage point, benefits to all from the special insight and talent of some, technical assistance, and religious guidance. New patterns keep emerging before the old are understood and evaluated. The vocational fellowship could stem the gap and "be called to the new frontier to use its combined experience, judgment, and sensitized conscience to formulate an ethical opinion." [32]

The town and country parish in mid-20th-century America may be in a similar position as was Paul on the Damascus road. With startling suddenness and brilliance, the risen Christ confronted him with the words: "Saul, Saul, why do you persecute Me? It is hard for you, this kicking against the goad" (Acts 26:14 NEB). When the ox was yoked to the plow, a crossbar with little knives was set behind so that if the ox refused to obey but kicked, it would be reminded it was to work. Many "goads" dig into town and country parishes: the emptying countrysides with attendant problems of stagnation or decline for some and the ferment of rapid growth for others, the decline of small towns' power and vigor, the problem of shrinking incomes amid agriculture's abundance.[33] The social and economic shifts continue; those going through them feel their formerly stable world is like a crazy kaleidoscope, always coming up with new, unexpected patterns.

These goads of social and economic change can remind town and country parishes that in taking the yoke of Christ they assumed the responsibility of being His church where they are. They ought not romantically desire to turn back the clock, for they cannot go back to life as it was, and refusal to accept their presence is what presses the goads deeper. Rather, the goads will be beneficial if parishes in town and country will search more deeply to find who they are as church, if parishes will set their desire for stability on their Lord and not on institutional patterns, and if parishes will stop safeguarding their own existence and find their life by losing it in unexplored depths of mission service to both parish and world.

Notes

1. Robert Spike, *Safe in Bondage* (New York: Friendship Press, 1960), pp. 51, 52.

2. See note 33.

3. Max Lerner, *America as a Civilization* (New York: Simon and Schuster, 1957), p. 143.

4. Lerner, pp. 149, 150.

5. Arthur J. Vidich and Joseph Bensman, *Small Town in Mass Society*, Anchor Book (New York: Doubleday, 1960), pp. 80, 81.

6. Lerner, p. 151.

7. *Rurban*, a hybrid word, "refers to the blending and intermingling that goes on in the fringe area around our cities, where rural and urban cultures meet and mix." — Shirley E. Greene, *Ferment on the Fringe: Studies of Rural Churches in Transition* (Philadelphia: Christian Education Press, 1960), p. 15.

8. "New Thousands in Town and Country — Concern of the Church," in *Church in Town and Country*, George A. Van Horn, ed. (Chicago: National Lutheran Council, 1962), pp. 86, 87.

9. David Riesman, *The Lonely Crowd*, Anchor Book (New York: Doubleday, 1955), p. 122.

10. Ethelbert Stauffer, *New Testament Theology*, trans. John Marsh (New York: Macmillan, c. 1955), pp. 203, 204.

11. Spike, p. 9.

12. Vidich and Bensman, p. 36.

13. *The Silent Struggle for Mid-America: The Church in Town and Country Today*, E. W. Mueller and Giles C. Ekola, eds. (Minneapolis: Augsburg, 1963), p. 98.

14. Vidich and Bensman, p. 245.

15. Greene, p. 46.

16. H. Richard Niebuhr, *The Social Sources of Denominationalism*, Living Age Book (New York: Meridian, 1957), pp. 5, 6, 25.

17. Vidich and Bensman, pp. 251, 252.

18. Spike, pp. 63, 64.

19. D. T. Niles, *Upon the Earth* (New York: McGraw-Hill, 1962), pp. 77, 78.

20. This section owes much to Abbé G. Michonneau, *The Missionary Spirit in Parish Life* (Westminster, Md.: Newman, 1952), pp. 67—89.

21. Georges Bernanos, *The Diary of a Country Priest*, Image Book (New York: Doubleday, 1954), pp. 22, 23.

22. John Heuss, *Our Christian Vocation* (Greenwich, Conn.: Seabury, 1955), pp. 14, 15.

23. Victor Obenhaus, *The Church and Faith in Mid-America* (Philadelphia: Westminster, 1963), p. 23.
24. A sample of sociological techniques and theological undergirding of self-study may be gained from Reuben J. Schmidt's unpubl. essay, "The Mission of the Church in Town and Country Areas" (St. Louis: Board for Missions in North and South America, 1963).
25. *Christ and His Community in the World* (Chicago: National Lutheran Council, 1963), pp. 38, 39.
26. Tom Allan, *The Face of My Parish* (London: S. C. M., 1954), pp. 63 to 65.
27. Greene, p. 47.
28. Obenhaus, p. 70.
29. Greene, pp. 39—41.
30. In private correspondence.
31. Obenhaus, pp. 41—45 and 72—82.
32. *The Silent Struggle*, p. 96.
33. Sources for the sections "Greater Agricultural Productivity" and "Static or Declining Income":

    U. S. Dept. of Agriculture Yearbooks: *Power to Produce* (1960), *After a Hundred Years* (1962), *A Place to Live* (1963), Washington, D. C.: U. S. Government Printing Office.

    "Facts and Trends About the Rural Population," U. S. D. A., FES, RDPA 5 (11/62), Washington, D. C.

    "Recent Population Trends in the United States with Emphasis on Rural Areas," U. S. D. A., Agricultural Economic Report No. 23, ERS, Jan. 1963, Washington, D. C.

Death and Birth of the Parish

In The Suburbs

Roy Blumhorst

Death and Birth of the Parish

In The Suburbs

Death and birth imply sickness and health, yet, judged by the most obvious symptoms, no place seems less in need of diagnosis than the suburban parish. Here at least the church seems to be thriving. The empty cathedrals of the inner city and the deserted grounds of the rural parish may be signs of a fatal illness, but the neat contemporary structure of the suburban congregation is swarming with people. Antichurch resentment may be found in the dense metropolis and postchurch apathy in the stretches of the farmland, but in suburbia many people still seem to be in favor of the church. While other areas report dwindling membership, financial crises, and problems of leadership, suburban parishes continue to break records in growth, to thrive with talented people, and to have financial trouble only because of the size of their building program. Isn't the church successful at least in the suburbs if nowhere else? Isn't much of the criticism leveled at suburban congregations simply an indication of envy? Must a book like this not stretch a point to find serious need for death and birth in the suburbs?

Christ's denunciations of the Pharisees were not His way of indicating that they were necessarily worse than others; He just didn't want them to be deceived by external signs into thinking they were better. A look at suburban parishes indicates roughly the same problem. The externals can easily lead them into avoiding the basic questions of mission and purpose. The danger is not so much that they will soon fold up, but that in the midst of their success they will fail in the assignment given them by Christ. The purpose of this chapter is not to apply one more lashing to the often-beaten suburban church. We rather want to be aware that "success" is a term for industry and not for discipleship. Then we can go beneath the externals to the basic question: "Does our parish really represent the church in this place?" We want to ask the question, not because we are trying to save our neck but because we are the church and are under the obligation to serve not ourselves but Christ.

The Suburbs

A suburban parish serves a suburb. The suburb itself is a fairly recent development. Fortune magazine calls a suburb any census tract in the metropolitan area in which two thirds of the families own their own homes and both the income and number of children are above the national average. Some 20,000,000 people have moved to these fringes of metropolitan centers in the last 15 years.[1] What are suburbs like? A quick set of adjectives will give us an overview.

Separated

A suburb is *separated*. Perhaps the most obvious characteristic of suburbs is their narrow slice of humanity. Although the day of building 300 homes of identical size, shape, and cost may be passing to one which offers at least six modifications of the one design, the people inside the houses are still quite identical. Each suburb tends to have its own particular level ranging from the just-getting-started suburb through the comfortable to the exclusive, but within each grouping the people are highly similar. Suburbanization has been described as "a cream-separation process, whereby the better paid middle class is floated off by itself where it spends less on public welfare and more on its own desires." [2] Occupationally most of the people are professional or white-collar, with little of the rest of American humanity involved.

Isolated

A suburb is *isolated,* an obvious result of the process of separation. Whereas it might have once been true that community included residence, work, and recreation all in one area, this is not the case in suburbia. Work is usually at the end of an express-way or commuter run. Culture and recreation are often specialized activities in nearby metropolitan centers. Left for the suburban area is the function of residence-houses upon houses with only the educational and minor marketing functions still kept local. The rapid growth of major shopping centers increases the separation from the downtown area. In many ways this isolation is deliberate. Americans move to the suburbs not simply from a need for space — it's often still available in the center of the city — but from a desire to escape the evils of an industrial society. The move is an attempt to recapture the American dream of the small town with heavy emphasis on family and home life. The result, however, is a large measure of isolation, teen-agers who have no real concept of work because they live only in residential areas, adults who ride through problem areas and talk about the city which they adjoin, but have little real involvement in either.

Laminated

Taken as a whole, however, the suburban area is a *laminated* one. Even though an individual suburb may be narrowly con-sistent in values, incomes, and class, it may well adjoin one com-pletely different. Trailer courts abound, and new subdivisions with either much cheaper or much more expensive homesites are built. Like a piece of plywood a suburban complex thus has highly distinct communities pushed side by side. A suburban parish oriented too narrowly to one class can miss the mobile home courts or the exclusive set of 100 houses nearby.

Uprooted

A suburb is *uprooted*. Because it represents either the beginning or the middle or the end of a long journey upward, the suburb is largely inhabited by people on the move. Although some suburbanites are simply refugees from the inner city, very many follow a different pattern. An enterprising man in a small town is promoted to a position in a metropolitan area; he moves into an adjoining suburb; on his second promotion he moves out to a regional office; he returns later as an executive living in a more exclusive suburb. As a result few suburban children attend the same school for eight years.

Educated

A suburb is *educated*. Probably nowhere is the value of education more appreciated than in the suburb. Education has been the vehicle of advancement in America, and the suburbanite knows it more than anyone else. Many of the men and women share a college background, and for those who don't have it education is the great goal for their children. Education, either possessed or desired for one's children, ranks high in suburban values.

Adjusted

A suburb is *adjusted* — or at least spends much of its time trying to be. The people who inhabit it are trying to realize a dream, a dream to be enjoyed. Enjoyment precludes dissatisfaction, rebellion, disenchantment. Andrew Greeley outlines the problems of adjustment for suburban youth, suburban men, and suburban women.[3]

The adjustment shows up most strikingly in the young people. Suburban youth have a freedom impossible for previous generations or other areas. Yet in the main they tend to be conservative, domestic, studious, accepting the values and goals of the adults around them. Except for widely publicized flings, this group — which by nature might be expected to be more visionary and idealistic — is quite adjusted.

The suburban husband has to be adjusted too. He probably will be culturally oriented to think of working hours as much more important than leisure and to think of his occupational role as paramount to family, religious, or political activities. But with this inner orientation he will have superimposed the insistence that family comes first and that the only real happiness lies there. There may be real problems arising from conflicts between his moral code and the attainment of "success." In these tensions, however, the prime requirement is to adjust, to resolve the problem or be considered a failure, one who "couldn't handle it." So he is eager to be successful but must not appear so; he is enthusiastic about his work, but he must emphasize that family comes first. He must adjust, even though the rigors of adjustment generate tensions upon his tensions.

The suburban wife is not exempt from the struggle either. Possessing a high level of education, possibly a college degree, she had her career ended by marriage and the need to rear the children. She looks at her decreased importance in the world and calls herself "just a housewife." She is smart enough to know that the endless community projects and child-sponsoring chores are still not quite the same as the role of her husband, and so she may feel unnecessary. Yet she too must adjust, throw herself into the community, and respond happily to the role assigned her.

Realized

Yet with all these attributes the suburbanite is one who has many of his dreams *realized*. The prospects for living, the freedom of his position, and the potential of his situation dare not

103

be minimized. Articles may bewail the suburbs, but few suburbanites want to leave them. Sin may abound, but so does grace. Our best view of the suburb would not write it off finally as tragedy, nor elevate it to the ideal, but would recognize that it is *different* — different not only geographically (in its newer houses, spacious lots and lawns, its trees, flowers, and shrubs), but different as a way of life from either the inner heart of the metropolis or the outer reaches of the country.

Potential of the Suburban Parish

The suburban parish is a place with potential but also a place challenging the church to face the changes. It could become a vibrant force in the 20th century, but unless it soon faces the magnitude of the changes around it, that force will be largely unused.

The suburban parish is a place where the ministry of the laity could most quickly reach its fullness. The accumulated ability, education, and resources available to the average member of a suburban congregation represent opportunities for real lay leadership. Suburban members can read, they can think, and they can act. They have been trained to do all of these. Many of them are eager to read, think, and act as members of Christ's body but have often grown weary under a situation which calls for none of these. Suburban men especially are in places of significance if not importance in business, politics, and society. The suburban parish can potentially reach these places.

If the early church spread by the persecution which sent Christians over the world, the suburban parish is in no less a potential position. The movement of members from one city to the next can mean that the adult training program of a little congregation in the suburbs will reach many places beyond its borders. Suburban congregations have the opportunity to receive a person in his weakness and send him on his way in strength, thus building the Kingdom in the world.

Potential also lies in the youth of suburban parishes. Most are not bound by a long historic tradition which is content to "leave things the way they are." The mere fact that they are recently organized makes them able to experiment and create in their approaches to the community. This youthfulness has another dimension too. Young couples and families abound. People who still are optimistic and energetic can be challenged to facing the 20th century instead of resenting it.

Struggle of the Suburban Parish

But there are signs that suburban parishes may not realize that the suburbs are different. Although new congregations abound, the newness too often consists only in the fact that they were recently organized. The cornerstone of the first unit may bear a number in the '50s or '60s, but the approach to the community sometimes is one designed to serve a rural congregation of the '20s or earlier. Here is where planned death and birth of the parish begin to assume importance.

There are signs that the suburban parish is trying to beat the world at its own game. The assumption seems to be that the parish is a formal structure whose one goal is to have people join and thus be saved. In pursuing this one goal the parish can employ all the techniques of industry — quick follow-up on new arrivals in the community, "servicing" of delinquent accounts, intensive work with "hot" prospects. When all of these are going well and the charts all have ascending lines, the parish is succeeding. Nowhere does this approach to the Kingdom reach more bizarre forms than in the suburbs, because here the competition (industry again) is most fierce. There aren't that many people in the acreage of a suburb in the first place, and there are often many churches. Denomina-

tions can compete too. The suburbanite chooses his church —
they all want him — on the basis of which one most adequately
meets his demands. Meantime parishioners are making their
ethical decisions, shaping their goals, influencing their society on
the basis of values completely unrelated to Jesus Christ.

There are also signs that the suburban parish is still striving
to be the center of community life. A congregation feels that
a complete program must include not just Word, Sacrament,
mutual fellowship, but also entertainment, activity, and diversion.
The suburban mother, who drives the children to school, attends
PTA, collects for charitable causes, helps in scouting activities,
and does all the shopping for the family, is sought out to join
congregational sewing circles, interest groups, and other societies
on the apparent assumption that she needs to "be involved."
She does indeed need to be involved with Christ, but has the
suburban parish done its thinking about the way that kind of
involvement should be accomplished?

And there is evidence that the suburban parish has not faced
the fact that it is part of a metropolitan area. The suburb may
be a deliberately separated and isolated area, but the kingdom
of God refuses to accept such restraints. The suburban congregation is thus forced to think through its context of responsibility. If it continues to let itself believe that its only interests
are those which lie within its geographical boundaries, it will
have an abbreviated role — to say the least.

The matter of building love between persons of different races
is probably the best current example. By accepting the parochial
view of its mission, the suburban congregation can easily avoid
its responsibility. Being concerned with its own clientele, it
ignores the fact that only several miles away live other members
of Christ's body with whom it is organically one. Separation
does havoc to Paul's "when one member suffers all suffer."
Congregations wonder how the message of Christ can be given

106

any relevance in their kind of setting, while all around them metropolitan problems are crying for involvement. A suburban congregation can easily be trapped into accepting no more responsibility than what it sees from the church window — residences of private dwellings, and no more. It is no secret that the inner city is one of the most demanding and pressing fields for the Kingdom in our time, yet many suburban congregations think of the inner city in the same way they do of "foreign missions."

Death and birth of the parish must be faced also by the suburban parish for two reasons: its potential and its changed situation. The church must adjust to the changes. If it ignores them and continues a purely traditional program, it will soon lose its influence and decay. The suburban parish may come uncomfortably close to the Biblical Sardis: "I know your works; you have the name of being alive, and you are dead" (Rev. 3:1). What we desire in suburbia is not more success, but more discipleship.

Death and Birth for Suburban Parishes

Some would suggest that the suburban parish die, so that new forms of ministry might emerge. Chapter 1 has explained our reasons for staying with the parish. We believe that the necessary death and birth can be accomplished within the parish and that the parish can continue its role as the local representation of the church of Jesus Christ.

But this assumption places on parish leaders the call to permit and promote that death and birth or, to put it sociologically, to analysis and change. To put it theologically, the leaders have the task of urging corporate repentance and new life. How shall they approach the task? Shall they kill off all that is old and jump at anything new? Obviously not. This would be simple murder. Or should they turn to the sociologists and let them write the program? To do this would be to abandon their responsibility to God. Repentance doesn't work that way. Repentance happens when one puts himself under the Word and thus is led by the Spirit to change. A congregation is carrying out the rhythm of death and birth when it reexamines itself under the Word, letting die what doesn't fit and letting rise what the Spirit wills.

Obviously this kind of work must be done in each parish by its people. As the parish leaders engage in such examination, a set of approaches is developed which assumes responsibility to God and meets the kind of community the parish serves. No gimmicks or set programs can substitute for this exciting activity.

Without destroying the local parish's challenge we would now try to set forth some generalizations of death and birth in the suburb. They may point the way for some parishes and give possibilities. They can in no way be a manual on what to do. Our approach will be what we've just described, starting with what the Word is saying and looking at where we now stand. We will note a number of Biblical directives and derive implications for death and birth in suburban congregations.

In the Approach to a Community

Christian faith is commitment to Jesus Christ. Christ's approach to the disciples was simple. He said "Follow Me." This provides an insight into the nature of Christian faith. Christianity never intends to be an exercise in religion aimed at providing peace of mind and satisfying man's inner needs. Many religions attempt that. The roots of that kind of religion are in man. Nor is Christianity an exercise aimed at helping man make himself good. It writes that goal off as impossible.

The Christian proclamation is that in Christ God became incarnate in the world, the real world. In the world He called men to Himself to rescue them from being natural enemies of

God no matter how moral, or good, or secure they might feel. Christian faith is the positive response to that call. The disciple makes this commitment. "Indeed I count everything as loss because of the surpassing worth of knowing Christ Jesus my Lord." (Phil. 3:8)

The faith aspect of Christianity, brought about by the working of the Holy Spirit, is stressed by Robert Raines: "For Christianity is not primarily a creed, though we must spell out in systematic fashion what we do believe; nor is Christianity primarily a code of ethics, though we must clarify and pursue the social implications of our faith. Christianity at heart is a *total personal commitment to Jesus Christ*. It is nothing other than, or less than, a personal relationship with Him. This relationship requires conscious decision on our part." [4]

The New Testament word *church* denotes those who are called out. It is the work of the Holy Spirit who calls people to consciously commit themselves to Jesus Christ. With this perspective we accept the limitations of a Christian parish. It is not in existence to satisfy all of men's needs, nor is it aimed primarily at meeting them. It is in existence to face people inside and outside its membership with Jesus Christ. It has a prophetic role, calling into question those fictions and activities of men which deny Him. [5] It has a healing role, effecting reconciliation between men and God and men and each other.

This change is often called conversion. "We *had* to become new persons. Our old selves simply couldn't and wouldn't go and witness in the world. We have discovered in our own experience the necessity of conversion." [6] Such emphasis on conscious decision for Christ is embarrassing in the suburbs, as elsewhere. Ours is so often a place of noncommitment; we like religion at a distance. We would rather build character without discipleship or have our Christianity by osmosis. People may not resist church membership, but they decidedly resist change.

Yet the Christian parish is committed not to increasing membership but to turning people to Christ. The main task of the church is to provide the conditions and circumstances in which God may call people to a definite, deliberate commitment to follow Jesus Christ.

So what must die in the suburban parish? The approach to people which emphasizes that the parish merely exists to serve them. One sometimes gets the impression that the church is running on a platform which says, "We can do more for you than anyone else." Publicity blurbs, invitation brochures, and religious advertising stress, "Come to our church because we are friendlier, we have more to offer you, you will be happier." It is an approach which appeals to suburbanites. They are accustomed to being king and demanding what best suits them. But it is an approach which distorts the calling activity of Christ, which asks not for the privilege of filling man's needs but for man's commitment. A parish cannot simply plan to satisfy the members and their particular desires. The question is not, "How can God be more useful to me?" The question is rather, "How am I useful to Christ?" This question can be woven into the planning and goals of a parish.

Suburbanites, like all people, like to follow the rule: first me, then you, last God. For this reason nothing short of conversion and commitment can accomplish the church's goal.

Andrew Greeley proposes a "spirituality for suburbanites" which might well put specific meaning to the commitment.[7] He suggests first of all *self-denial*. Suburban affluence can easily become suburban avarice. Can a person keep balance among all the gadgets without finding it necessary to deny himself some of them? The spirituality would include *generosity*. The suburban person can easily fit into Jesus' story about the rich man and his success. Jesus concluded with a warning to those who lay up treasures for themselves and are not rich toward God. Greeley also suggests real *engagement* with the world. It is easy for the suburbanite to write off the slums, the bad politics, and the neighboring communities as no problem for him. Commitment to Jesus Christ will not let him off so easily. Finally, Greeley proposes an emphasis on *reading*. If suburban people have both the ability and the inclination to read, can we not foster a higher level of Christian commitment by making such literature available? In many parishes the only library is composed of donated books in dusty corners. But a library is not the only possibility. One role for the pastor would be to suggest literature to the people with the goal of deeper commitment in mind.

In the Relation Between Congregations

God creates the church. The temptation of suburban Christians is to see the church as man's creation. They can remember how it was. A group of like-minded people got together and decided it would be nice to have a congregation in the neighborhood. They then went to work, calling a pastor, procuring a site, and setting up an organization. First we have a group of Christians, then we have a church. Grateful recognition is given God in the printed history, but the prominent characters are all men. This concern may seem like an unnecessary chicken-or-egg quibble about words until we face some of the implications. The resistance of official boards to any change in the institution, the pride with which members discuss what "we have done," and the selfishness about "our church" are not to be overlooked.

A little Bible group studying the Book of Ephesians came up with a startling discovery. "Why, it wasn't our idea at all!" they concluded with genuine amazement. Parishes arise because God the Holy Spirit is creating the church. They accordingly are not "our" churches and they are not answerable to us.

If God creates the church and it is His church and the parish is but a local representation of the church, then certainly the insistence on local autonomy must die. It is easy for the suburban congregation to assume that it is off in its own little corner of the world and free from any real relation to the parishes elsewhere. Any contact which it has with others will be purely optional and secondary. Yet in its very backyard will be congregations which are not just "needy" but are the real potential of its mission. The suburban congregation could be involved in the real mission outreach of the church simply by getting deeply involved with these congregations. If an inner-city and a suburban parish were to become part of each other, the matching of resources with burdens would undoubtedly be both exciting to the members and beneficial to the Kingdom. The truth of the matter is that they *are* one. Read Ephesians if you don't believe it. God intends it and the complexity of the supercity demands it. Those denominations which stress local autonomy for the congregation must somehow come up with better approaches to the interdependence of the parishes. In metropolitan areas this interdependence must especially relate suburban, mid- and inner-city congregations in a joint mission.

An overdeveloped sense of local autonomy also is in conflict with suburban mobility. Only a small percentage of suburban members will spend their life within the confines of one parish. "Mobility demands a wider vision of the church." [8] When the holy catholic church is too closely identified with the local congregation, the moving members are ill equipped to retain their primary loyalty to the universal church and leave behind the local representations. It should be possible for the member to leave one parish and join another without any great break in his joys and participation. Instruction for church membership would thus emphasize primarily this universal church and not the local congregation. The goal of the congregation is not to build a little kingdom but to win people for the Lord Jesus Christ.

Sometimes Lutheran parishes are involved in a consolidated

school. Strict measures are often taken to assure each congregation that it will lose none of its autonomy. Each pastor comes in to instruct "his" children separately. Can these practices be justified in the light of the kind of loyalty Christians are trying to build? Why cannot one pastor instruct all the children together, dividing by age units rather than congregations?

Interdependence also applies to the relation of suburban congregations to one another. It's popular to criticize the government for its overlapping agencies in which a highway commission destroys the most recent work of the park and conservation agency. But what about the waste in suburban churches? School buses overlap, newcomers are called on by two congregations of the same denomination, and duplication of effort is needlessly made. Whatever correctional measures are taken by way of suburban planning should both conserve effort and testify to the interdependence of the parishes.

If God creates the church, then the structures with which men operate are all secondary and temporary. When we look at the scattered glimpses of the church in the New Testament we see no standardized and rigid code of operation; we find practical approaches to the situation as they found it. The people were pursuing the mission and did whatever seemed best to fit the time. There seemed to be little awareness that they were setting precedents or creating patterns for the rest of time. They frankly were not so sure that time would last that long. Because God's created church is a creation made up of men, changes are bound to come.

We have mentioned some of the distinctive features of the suburbs. A suburban parish cannot value constitution, form of government, or any other tradition above needed death and birth. For example, the traditional pattern of church government may be a group of all men over 21 meeting once a month in the evening. This may be unworkable in the suburb because of the

113

number of men who work evenings, the number of men who travel consistently, and the number of men who see that it doesn't take 40 people to make a decision and therefore cannot see any real necessity for their attendance. In such a case that tradition might well die and a more representative, workable plan rise. This has often already taken place.

In the Relation Between Members

The church is people. This perspective is especially essential in the life of the parish. The New Testament encourages Christians to bear one another's burdens, to admonish one another, and most of all to assume that one belongs to the other. Missing from the New Testament is any implication that people are secondary to the institution. The people *are* the parish in all their weakness as well as all their strength. So it is assumed that there will be the weak as well as the strong, the inert as well as the active; one of the chief purposes of the congregation is that these might serve one another — especially that the strong might serve the weak. Only those who by their open rejection have separated themselves from the body of Christ are to be excluded. The weak may be embarrassing and they may constitute a burden, but they are one of the very reasons for which the parish exists: that the strong might serve the weak.

Yet frequently pastors and zealous leaders try to build an "ideal" congregation, in which there is perfect harmony. By striving to create on earth what finally is given only by God, they subordinate the people of the parish to the institution. Thus leaders may complain about the kind of members who belong to the parish or wish that they didn't have them. They do not realize that these are the people whom God has given the parish, for whom He is to be thanked, and to whom they are asked to minister. In building the "ideal," people are divided into categories by the way they are helping or hindering the program. They are seen as allies or obstacles rather than as brothers and opportunities.

The practice of "cleaning up the rolls" for the sake of efficiency must be called into question. To legalistically exclude the weak brother is to exclude Christ's opportunity for us to serve the weak. The practice of having a standard set of procedures mechanically starting with a form letter and concluding with a notice of termination seems much more a method of efficient business operation than of personally and lovingly dealing with one who is weak. To identify the weak brother with the unrepentant sinner of Matt. 18 is a practice not worthy of the parish, which is committed to bringing repentance and life to a world of sinners.

Instead the parish can be a place where the few serve the many. It does not need to aim each program at the complete membership but should first of all enable the few to accept their ministry to the many. The 50 percent of the young people who constitute the youth group don't have to begin by complaining that half aren't in attendance and try gimmicks to get them. They can rather determine what they can do for their fellow young people to build them up in the fellowship. The small groups in Bible classes are not necessarily a sign of failure. They can be the nucleus which strengthens the others by their growth. The problem is that often the little groups already in existence are ignored or given poor food for growth while massive programs aimed at total participation sap all the energy of the leaders.

In Fellowship

The people are joined in a body for *fellowship*. If the emphasis in the church is not institution but people, then we gain new insight into the insistence of the New Testament that the church is a body. A body is a living organism with complete interrelation of its parts. The New Testament uses human analogies rather than institutional ones. The words are not promote, administer,

115

and succeed, but serve, teach, preach, suffer. The emphasis is on the Holy Spirit working through people, people who are joined to one another as one. There is fellowship, but this fellowship is not just a romantic togetherness. It is a kind of togetherness which must be understood. Members of Alcoholics Anonymous have a distinct fellowship with one another though one may be a business executive and another a day laborer. Their unity is the common determination to fight a common problem. The Christian church has a similar fellowship. The common Head is Jesus Christ, the common source of nourishment is Word and Sacrament, and the common goal is growth.

The congregation often gets derailed in its fellowship because it tries to build on nature instead of the gift of divine grace. It thinks that getting people together to do something — anything in fact — will be fellowship. It wonders that nothing vital seems to happen. Forming groups around purely human interests or human capabilities may actually divide the body. Thus a ladies' bridge group would automatically exclude those ladies who don't play bridge. Groups and organizations which require too many social and educational characteristics for membership are hardly creating fellowship. Men do not share natural characteristics in the church; they share grace. It may be painful to realize there certainly are societies in congregations which are interest groups and nothing more. They are hardly bringing fellowship into being.

In the parish fellowship must be based on grace. The members share a common fight with sin, a common witness to the world, and a common source of life; why cannot their fellowship be based on this? As a prime example of the difference between nature and grace, we might learn from an experience given by George Webber. In bringing men from two highly different congregations together, the matter of introductions might have immediately disrupted fellowship. Had each man indicated his name and occupation, the great difference between the bank president and the unemployed laborer sitting next to him would have stood out boldly. Instead the leader asked each one to give his name and to state how he had come to be a Christian. All were on the same terms as matters of faith, the Word, and grace came to the fore.[9]

The parish needs its small groups, but they need primarily to be groups which share grace and not nature. Peter directs, "As each one has received the gift, so serve it to one another" — and the gift is nothing other than grace. As a way of implementing the relating of societies to grace and not to nature we might use four basic questions. (1) How does this group either equip the members of the body for their witness or send them on it? (These are finally the purposes of the parish.) (2) Upon what common denominator does it build — is it one of nature or grace? (3) Does the group enable its members to withdraw from the other members of the congregation, or does it give them a ministry to them? (4) How do the members grow in their relation to one another by membership in the group? On the basis of these questions the group rises or dies.

In the Mission of the Church

The body is a mission. "Ye are the salt of the earth, the light of the world." "As My Father has sent Me, even so send I you." The suburban congregation is not where it is only for the mutual protection of its members. Salt, light, and leaven are penetrative elements. The church is God's reach into the world, lighting it, preserving it, changing it. It follows that the parish cannot reduce this mission to mere increase, although this is not to be despised. Its penetration will also include the many facets of community where Christ needs to be represented.

Admittedly the relation between church and world is not easily maintained. "The temptation . . . is either so to separate itself from the world (society) that it has little communication with it, or so to identify" with it that it has no challenge to offer.[10] It will find its balance when it recalls two basic facts. One is that God created the world (so the distortion of sin dare never let us write off anything or anyone around us). The other is that God redeemed the world and that reconciliation is being brought to the world by way of the church. "I do not pray that Thou shouldst take them out of the world, but that Thou shouldst keep them from the evil one. . . . As Thou didst send Me into the world, so I have sent them into the world" (John 17:15, 18). The parish exists because of the world; it is there to bring the world reconciliation.

The world is the community in which the parish lives. There is thus "something damning about a congregation when men and women can live within its shadows . . . without knowing anything about it except that it is a church and that some people go there on Sundays." [11] The whole program and life of the parish must be related to the community in which it lives. T. E. Matson's questions, which we have adapted, are good for a suburban parish to use in trying to be a mission in its community:

1. Is our congregation meeting the challenges and changes of our community? Are we facing the particular problems of people around us and reflecting the new features of our locality?

2. Are our programs and activities outdated for our kind of community? Were they devised for a different area, or situation, or group?

3. Does the total parish program proclaim the Gospel in a way that people around us can understand?

4. Would it actually make any difference to the community if our congregation went out of existence?

The congregation would be interested in facts such as these:

1. Who are the people who live within the parish neighborhood or community? . . .

2. What is the religious practice of the community? . . .

3. What is the depth of Christian thinking in the community? . . .

4. What is the self-image of the congregation? . . .

5. How do the members evaluate the congregation's attitude toward its neighborhood and people? [12]

This evaluation would take into consideration the lamination of the suburban areas and the realization that the trailer courts and expensive subdivisions are also a part of the mission.

In the Function of Laymen

The layman is the bridge. Hopefully we have begun to realize that in the Christian vocabulary layman does not mean amateur. We have begun to appreciate that what we have in a congregation is not a pastor and his clients. The Reformation heritage of the royal priesthood has long raised the cry that every person is responsible directly to God, but this is only half the picture. Every person is *necessary* to God. In 1 Cor. 12 we are reminded how useless a body made up of nothing but eyes or ears would be. A congregation made up of nothing but preachers would be just as senseless. A preacher fulfills one function; there are equally vital functions which he does not fulfill.

What kind of role does the layman have in the congregation? The lowest level of congregational thinking seems to be that laymen exist only to call and support the pastor. They project him into the community. "We'll send the pastor."

The level above this seems to be that the layman can help the pastor. The pastor is seen as overburdened, pressed for time. Thus minor tasks are found for the layman, "to free the pastor." Thus the chief role of the layman still seems to be helping the pastor. If Eph. 4 is taken seriously, this approach must die. The congregation must not be abbreviated into the functions of a pastor and his helpers.

119

The real function of the layman is that of being the church in the world. This function is not always possible for the preacher. After all, he does not ride the commuter trains, sit at the bridge tables, belong to a union, or run a business. Reaching people in all walks and places of life is the task of the person who is in all walks and places of life, the layman. His role is clear enough; he is the church penetrating the world of work, of leisure, and of residence with the witness to Jesus Christ.

For this reason less time needs to be spent in the parish on finding something for the layman to do and more time on preparing him for the task he already has. All kinds of possibilities can rise from this death and birth.

The chief problem of congregations seems to be that they do not take this role seriously. It is easier to have the layman fulfill his ministry by doing only the necessary routine services which keep the congregation going than by putting teeth into an advance on the community. As one laymen put it, "If I were to really be a Christian in this business I'd lose my shirt in a week." The problem is not finding this man something to do, but preparing him for what he already should be doing.

In Worship

The congregation gathers to worship. We can think, then, of a congregation as the people of God gathering and scattering. They gather to worship, to be trained, and to be supported. They scatter into the community. This scattering we have already discussed in the look at "mission" earlier. How about the gathering?

Corporate worship is essential to the parish. Worship is response to God. It is a response which acknowledges His rightful place as Lord. It is a response made possible in Jesus Christ. It is because the people have been reconciled to God that they can worship God. When the group of people gathers on Sunday morning, this is already the realization of God's work. They are

120

the redeemed and they are gathered in His name. All around people may be cutting lawns or washing cars, but God's Word has not returned to Him void. There are people responding. Their first response is worship, and it is a necessary response. But this worship is also corporate, bringing the "body" back into focus. In addition to having other shortcomings, listening to a religious program on the radio in place of attending worship services neglects the fellow believers to whom one is joined. Paul severely censured the Corinthian congregation for not paying due attention to the body of believers. As people gather on Sunday morning there is significance in their gathering. Common response to God must be made because they are at one with one another. During the week they may be scattered through the metropolis, but in corporate worship the unified group becomes most visible. The climax of that gathering is the participation in Holy Communion. Here the fellowship with Him and with one another is in its most concrete and noticeable form. Corporate worship is essential to the parish because it is both worship and corporate. Dare we suggest death to our pattern of worship? Isn't this one field where the older the tradition the more valuable the form? Contrasting the liturgy with what comes over our TV set is no doubt of value — in church we are not pursuing men but standing before God.

It is difficult to get modern man involved in ancient liturgy. Twentieth-century man, for example, is bombarded on every hand by the sensuous. Freedom and ecstasy seem to be identified with living in the satisfaction of one's senses. The liturgy is restrained and restraining upon man. The TV set pushes for the quick point — the one-minute commercial, the 15-minute "complete news of the day." The liturgy moves slowly and subtly. Modern communication has practically no ability to convey agreed-upon symbols. The liturgy is rich in symbolism and requires imagination on the part of the participant. Modern communication

121

moves directly to the point, the liturgy moves indirectly. Modern man is primarily machine oriented, the liturgy is mostly nature centered.[18]

Two possibilities would seem to be in order for the suburban parish. One is that the parish not simply be devoted to resurrecting old forms and orders. Old forms should be judged on the same basis as new ones: what is the theology, meaning, and value to the group which is using them? The current development in Europe of a church year which takes into consideration modern man's questions about the existence of God, his need for emphasis on creation, for example, would be the kind of change which keeps the liturgy in touch with the person using it.

The other necessity for the suburban parish is deliberate preparation for worship. A good place to begin is in the meetings which the parish holds during the week. As long as these are opened with haphazard Bible readings and prayer, bad training obtains. Even though it is for a few brief moments, the time should be used to set the entire meeting in an atmosphere of worship; a secondary benefit would be developing the people in the art of worship itself. Lay leadership of this informal worship would more quickly prepare laymen for their response on Sunday morning too.

The instruction can be done in the adult education groups and in the morning service. It is most important that the congregation deliberately accept the responsibility of preparing its members for worship. When properly developed, worship can be the time when man is freed from his mass culture, at least in part, and finds something completely different and edifying.

In the Educational Program

The congregation gathers to train. For some reason Bible study, training, fellowship, and prayer are often completely separated in the functions of the congregation. Bible study seems often to be primarily aimed at more knowledge about our faith. The learning of information is central even when much is made of little groups and discussion-type classes. Training is reserved for special programs of the congregation — evangelism or stewardship, for example. Prayer is usually formal and appended to whatever the specific purpose of the meeting happens to be. Fellowship is whenever we get together for none of these.

They cannot be separated. James reminds us that simply looking in the Word and going our way will result in forgetting what we have seen. Much Bible study fails to penetrate beneath the surface, not because it was poorly prepared but because it wasn't seen as training or done with mutual witness or accompanied with prayer. The same interlocking characteristics could be demonstrated for the other three activities. When the Word is heard, witnessed to one another, and commended to prayer, we have a group which is being trained.

The small groups described by both Webber and Raines are perhaps the best examples of a uniting of all these functions. Corporate worship and small groups are the two foci of these parishes. The small group is the focus enabling the congregation to equip people for their task. The group cannot be designed simply to make people more pious or simply to instill more knowledge about faith. It exists to do even more than stimulate faith or create fellowship. It must go beyond all this and prepare people for the mission of the church.

Such a small group could meet twice a month for the nine winter months in the homes of members. There is no attempt to deliberately structure the groups by age or interest — they are not based on nature but grace. The period begins with a 15-minute devotion, then continues for about an hour and a half with discussion of the material. Suggested two-year cycle for material: introduction to the Bible, Gospel According to Mark, Acts, Ephesians, Galatians, or 1 Corinthians. The end of the period is then shared prayer. The members of the group try to pray for specific persons and concerns in their community.[14] The intercessory prayer of the group members will be some of their finest training, for it is here that they learn to speak without embarrassment to God and about God. It is in praying for specific people that they find themselves being sent to them.

Such a group has all the essential elements: Bible study, training, prayer, and fellowship. The same structure can be used with a series of teachers' meetings, a special retreat, special groups, boards of elders, and other small groups already in the parish.

Conclusion

No kit of instructions can be given the suburban parish for shaping its presence in the community. More valuable is the time spent by its leaders asking the right questions and then setting out to implement the answers. Our conclusion is therefore a simple restating of the general questions for possible consideration by leaders of a parish.

1. Does our parish strive to satisfy our members or to call them to specific commitment to Jesus Christ? Does it take conversion and commitment, inside and outside the membership, seriously?

2. Are we accepting the mission of the metropolitan area? Are we training people to think of the church in terms of the whole supercity instead of emphasizing our own little bailiwick? Do we preserve patterns and traditions which may no longer be useful to the Kingdom?

3. What is our approach to removing members? Are we clear about our reasons and are they the ones given in Scripture?

4. What is the reason for each society in our parish? Does it fit the New Testament idea of fellowship?

5. What is our relation to the community?

6. What is the function of the layman in our parish?

7. Why do we use our particular forms of worship? What is our training program for worship?

8. What kind of enabling groups do we have? Do they combine Word, training, prayer, and fellowship?

A congregation need not fear death and birth. It is out of this process that life continues to pass from one generation to the next.

Notes

1. Andrew J. Greeley, *The Church and the Suburbs* (New York: Sheed and Ward, 1959), p. 29.
2. Edward Higbee, *The Squeeze* (New York: William Morrow, 1960), p. 100.
3. Andrew Greeley, passim.
4. Robert Raines, *New Life in the Church* (New York: Harper and Brothers, c. 1961), p. 41.
5. Peter L. Berger, *The Precarious Vision* (New York: Doubleday, 1961), p. 65 et passim.
6. Robert Raines, p. 19.
7. Andrew Greeley, pp. 191 ff.
8. Theodore Matson, *Edge of the Edge* (New York: Friendship Press, 1961), p. 72.
9. George Webber, *God's Colony in Man's World* (New York: Abingdon, 1960), p. 66.
10. Theodore Matson, p. 22.
11. Ibid., pp. 110—114.
12. Loc. cit.
13. Andrew Greeley, p. 192 ff.
14. Adapted from Robert Raines, pp. 85—87.

Death and Birth of the Parish

IN THE CITY

Kenneth R. Young

✠

Death and Birth of the Parish

❧

IN THE CITY

Blessed be the God and Father of our Lord Jesus Christ, who has blessed us in Christ with every spiritual blessing in the heavenly places, even as He chose us in Him before the foundation of the world, that we should be holy and blameless before Him. He destined us in love to be His sons through Jesus Christ, according to the purpose of His will, to the praise of His glorious grace, which He freely bestowed on us in the Beloved. In Him we have redemption through His blood, the forgiveness of our trespasses, according to the riches of His grace which He lavished upon us. For He has made known to us in all wisdom and insight the mystery of His will, according to His purpose which He set forth in Christ as a plan for the fullness of time, to unite all things in Him, things in heaven and things on earth. (Eph. 1:3-10)

In this section from Ephesians we learn that God's plan is to unite all things in Christ. How is His plan to be carried out? In and through the church, the one body of Christ, the followers of Jesus all over the world. As he develops the theme of oneness in his letter to the Ephesians, the apostle Paul explains that the church is the place where and the means by which God is carrying out His plan. That plan will be accomplished in the fullness of time.

Two out of every three Americans now live in metropolitan

areas. Both the percentage and the number will increase in the future. The areas themselves will grow geographically. At the heart of each area is a city or a cluster of cities, surrounded by suburbs. Many of the suburbs are in reality smaller cities, perhaps in turn developing their own outlying residential areas. Each metropolitan area is a unit, though even these units may lose their individuality as one area merges into another and an economic region is formed. Millions of people are living more and more closely together and are more and more dependent on one another. Thus interdependent city living is now the pattern for most Americans.

Bearing in mind the oneness in Christ which God wants throughout His creation (the oneness which exists in the church and is to be fostered within the church and through the church) and the urban environment in which so many people live, we shall consider briefly the life and work of the people of God within contemporary cities. After reviewing some of the main characteristics of cities and their impact on people and congregations, we shall consider the response of parishes to the cities in which they are located. This response to date has not brought God's plan to completion. All things are not yet united in Christ. His people are eager to do their full share in this process. Changes in the world must be met with changes in the parishes. And since some of those changes in the urban world are nothing short of revolutionary, the parishes are confronted with a powerful challenge. They are compelled to reexamine themselves, their life and God-given mission. They must be willing to change — even to change drastically — as the Holy Spirit leads. They dare not preserve those elements of their past that ought to be ended forever. They dare not suppress the new life the Spirit is seeking to give. We consider, therefore, the death and birth of the parish in the city.

The Modern City

First consider the setting of the city within today's world. The city is not isolated. Though it serves as the environment for millions, it is itself set into an environment. That environment could be studied and described in many ways and portrayed in larger and larger circles until the entire world is included. And this *is* the city's setting — nothing less than the entire world!

But what sort of world? A world in which advancing human knowledge and skills have brought an avalanche of change — some change bringing blessings for millions, some filling millions with fear — all of it coming so quickly and voluminously that it seems wholly capable, literally, of burying all human society. It is a world striving for the stars of the sky and dipping into the depths of the sea; yet it is unable to govern itself peaceably and does not care deeply when children go hungry. A world of turmoil and transition is taking new shape through processes labeled urbanization, industrialization, and bureaucratization. It is a world in which changes are so drastic that violent terms are used to describe them: Negro revolution, population explosion, political upheaval, commercial cataclysm. In this world distance has been eliminated by modern means of communication and transportation; it is one world conceived by science but born so prematurely that it has not yet learned the difficult art of living. It is a lawless world in which some work for the World Court, a material-minded world in which abstract art prevails, a pleasure-pursuing world in which monasteries are yet a model for millions, a proficient world whose skyscrapers stand while fountain pens fall apart, a godless world where millions give spiritual allegiance to the state while others pursue the old pagan gods and Americans turn to "religion-in-general," a college-bound world committed to comic strips, a parliamentary-procedure world where demonstrators make the decisions outdoors, a United Nations world overrun by nationalism, and a place where Americans and West Germans diet while East Germans and Indians starve. Over all this confused world hangs The Threat, the apparently imminent conflict between East and West.

Now turn to the city. Some would rather not. Some reject the city, regarding it as a symbol of evil. Others fashion it into an idol. Is the city a gift of God or deception from the devil? All depends on our attitudes toward it and the use we make of it. Our American heritage readily misleads us here. We have come from the forest, the frontier, the farm, and then from the small town. We held the opinion that Europe was crowded, urban, and artificial, while we were open, rural, and natural. We were swept along in the streams of industrialization, and with the help of hard-working immigrants we built our cities, too. They became magnets for millions while remaining centers of contradiction. Visions of the city beautiful clashed with earthy thoughts of the sinful city. To this day our love for cities seems mixed with suspicion, the flight to the suburbs perhaps expresses our deeper feelings, and most of those who care are concerned with reform.

But whatever one's attitude toward the city and city life, there is no doubt as to its importance. The city sways the world; its way of life is spreading everywhere. It carries threats and promises, advantages and disadvantages, evil and good. It is the source of the most prominent values of our culture, and at the same time it is the source of our most pressing problems. Whether for good or evil, whether one hates it or loves it, the city demands attention.

It is large and ever growing. To some observers cities seem to be sprawling so far that by A. D. 2,000 America will be short of space. Within the city, patterns are constantly shifting as changes occur in the use of the land — whether commercial, industrial, residential, recreational, educational, or institutional. Well-known today is the deterioration of the central or inner city. It is a port of entry for newcomers and a home for those who choose to live on the lower rungs of society's ladder, but a prison for those who are compelled to stay against their choice. But gradually some leave. They push out from the slums into neighborhoods slightly better. In turn they push others farther and farther out. The process reaches the periphery of the city, and millions have gone all the way to the suburbs and even beyond.

At the same time urban renewal has been attempted, primarily by the government. Vast residential areas have been demolished in the central city, huge low-cost housing projects have been erected in their place. In the very large cities the scene is complicated by the construction of expensive new housing not far from downtown business centers, so that there is also movement of people of high socioeconomic levels back to the city. Thus there are great movements of people; some come into the cities for the first time and some for the second; some move their location within the city — either by compulsion or by choice.

How else can we characterize a city? In addition to size and shifting patterns of population, the heterogeneity of the city is apparent. There is great variety among the people. Yet there are classes along social and economic lines, and other distinctions obtain according to race, color, language, or national origin. Many groups and individuals have not lost their identity in the great American melting pot. Along with this variety of people goes variety of activity. Diversity in choices is one of the unique characteristics of city life.

The city is devoted to industry and commerce. It has prospered, and it craves more and more of the material goods of life. The affluent society has been produced, and yet one out of every four does not share significantly in this affluence. It has prospered by means of technology and automation, and yet these very means have led to long lines of unemployed.

Along with its devotion to earning a living, the city is devoted to providing ways of spending that living. Housing, food, educa-

133

tion, safety, health, welfare, recreation — all of these needs are supplied in the city in various ways and to varying extents. Always there is inadequate quality and quantity — at least for some of the population. Increasing rates of crime, juvenile delinquency, mental disorders, and other forms of social pathology testify to this inadequacy. With shortening workweeks there is an increase in the need for recreation and other leisure-time activities, and the city provides all sorts of entertainment, amusement, and so on. It is a center of cultural development, supplying opportunities for all in the sciences and arts.

Good communications systems are essential within a city, and all of the means of mass media communications — newspapers, magazines, television, radio — are significant in shaping its life. Streets and expressways, a vast number of cars and trucks, buses and bicycles, trains and trolleys — all are evidence of the mobility within a city; at the same time, the furnishing of adequate means of transportation is one of the vexing problems of modern cities.

The larger and more complex the city the more important the role of government, and so as cities grow government becomes ever more dominant. Various writers have pointed out that the crucial decisions within cities are made by small groups of government and business leaders; the impact of their decisions comes down to the average citizen through a host of other people and institutions.

This, then, is a rough description of the modern city. It is a large, complex, diversified, busy, commercial, impersonal, ever-changing place in which people live highly interdependent lives.

Before proceeding, pause for a moment and consider several of the important segments of the city's population — important either from the standpoint of numbers or significance or both.

First, consider the Negroes, who are now 20 to 30 percent of the population in most of our larger cities and are expected to become the majority in seven out of 10 largest cities within the next 25 years. Wronged by their fellow Americans for centuries, confined largely to the inner city or low-cost projects (but leaving these when they are able), taking over the cities yet being swallowed up by them, choosing this way of life yet being unable to live it, holding the balance of political power but not yet using it for themselves — they are obviously a special group with special problems, a group (not wanting to be a group) which will play a prominent part in the destiny of our cities.

Second, remember the other minority groups within our population, and include here those language and national groups which have not yet been assimilated. Third, bear in mind all the newcomers to the city, whether Negro or Southern white or Spanish speaking. Fourth, think of the aged, an ever-growing segment of the city, having their own unique needs. Fifth, consider the children and youth, especially the young people having difficulty in school or at home or in the streets. Sixth, think of the unemployed, many of whom are rapidly becoming unemployable. Perhaps this is the best place to note that there is an ever-widening gap between those who are getting along satisfactorily and those who are not.

Influence of the City

A city is certain to have a great impact on its people. This impact flows from the nature of the city and the nature of its people. Some of its impact will be unpredictable and irrational, because that's the way people are. Yet it is possible to make some general statements. On the positive side it should certainly be noted that by their size and diversity cities are for many people stimulating and satisfying places in which to live. Otherwise they would not be there in such numbers. On the negative side it is apparent that large cities present many problems and dissatisfactions for many people. Otherwise they would not leave in such numbers as they do. The following description stresses some of the negatives because these are the factors creating the greatest problems for present-day city parishes.

The size and impersonality of the city makes for lives that are often shriveled and depersonalized. The individual, who is but a number among hundreds or even thousands, may lose his identity and come to think of himself as being very small and unimportant. There is a certain security in anonymity and an opportunity to avoid personal responsibility, but at the same time there is a loss of sense of self and personal value. There are so many people and so many choices that one is compelled to be uninterested in some of the other people and some of the other choices. Thus each individual has greater personal freedom and opportunity to choose, but in turn others are likely to be uninterested in him. He may join a group or support a cause, but this is often strictly temporary and implies no real involvement or giving of self. The individual may become lonely and lost amid crowds, yet he desires to conform and to remain largely hidden. He finds security in some sort of smaller group or subcommunity of individuals with whom he has something in common; in a large city even deviant characters can find others like themselves. But these subcommunities are based on only one or two shared characteristics, and the individual is then not a whole person. Thus lives become fragmented, and the individual sees neither himself nor other people as whole persons. It depends on the situation and the role being played at the moment: husband, parent, employee, church member, citizen, neighbor, or friend. As lives become fragmented, so does all of life.

As life becomes larger and more complex and more impersonal, the individual may well withdraw, lose his sense of personal involvement, and lose his feeling of community with his city. He may become frustrated, baffled, and helpless; yet he may also become highly suggestible and subject to manipulation by mass media communications. City life can too easily have this sort of impact on the person, so that in the end he is hardly a person at all.

Much has been written about family life in cities, particularly the negative impacts of city life upon families. There is indeed much family disorganization within cities; there are many forces that pull couples and families apart. Yet families have survived; they are capable of supplying city deficiencies regarding the identity and value of the individual. But one must recall the general fact that each year one out of every five American families changes its place of residence. Mobility has been woven into the American character. Though this brings new experiences and opportunities, it also destroys traditions, loyalties, and a sense of continuity and leaves a vague feeling of rootlessness and insecurity. One must also observe that our economic system and city life have made "acquisitive materialism" the ideal for millions of families. Though modern cities have a high and rising standard of living, the values placed on money and material goods have produced widespread craving for ever more comfort, pleasure, and status. Working mothers, dissatisfied teen-agers, and abandoned children are some of the significant results.

Along with fragmented life in general, also work has for many individuals become fragmented, secularized, and virtually meaningless. Technology demands ever-increasing specialization; modern marketing methods make corporations grow ever larger; automation leaves a trail of new problems. Shortened workweeks offer much more leisure oportunity, and cities provide a wide variety of activities. But many persons are not prepared to make wise choices and use their new leisure constructively so that it is re-creation. Television entertainment and spectator sports are more likely to be chosen than activities and hobbies that serve to develop the self. This is part of the pattern of noninvolvement, and it is carried over into civic activities and attitudes as well.

Though he is quick to complain about taxes and poor government, the average city dweller is equally quick to demand public services, while he himself is slow in being willing to serve. One just cannot fight city hall!

The Parish in the City

"Seek the welfare of the city where I have sent you into exile, and pray to the Lord on its behalf, for in its welfare you will find your welfare" (Jer. 29:7). So the prophet Jeremiah wrote to the people of God who had been taken to Babylon.

A parish is involved in its environment. A parish is not a building. A parish is people. Here we are thinking of the people described before: people who live in a city and who have been influenced by urban living. They are inextricably woven into the fabric of the city. They are shaped by the city and interact with their environment.

The city makes an impact on the parish. To be sure, we prefer to think of the impact the parish makes on the city. But we may as well admit that there is more that flows from the city to the parish than vice versa.

And here we do well to listen to all those who study the influences of the city on the parish. Although he undoubtedly overstates the case, Peter Berger, in *The Noise of Solemn Assemblies,* asserts that "the religious institution is irrelevant in terms of any of the powerful revolutionary forces" at work in cities. As part of his analysis he observes regretfully that "in a society which is increasingly urban in character, Protestant churchmen tend to look upon the city as essentially their enemy." In *The City Church — Death or Renewal* Walter Kloetzli writes:

> The city . . . is here to stay. It is the dominant influence in modern society, and in it are concentrated most of the pressing social problems of our day. In this environment 20th-century man must live, and within this ceaseless flux his institutional structures must

138

function with a certain degree of competence. The urban church is subject to the fluctuations, the tensions, and the changes of that sprawling giant, the city. Because so many churches have disbanded or have broken away, Protestantism seems to be failing or at best to be having only limited success in the city.[1]

What is the parish in the city like? Certainly each one is different and has its own history. Yet they can be grouped into general categories. Walter Kloetzli refers to these: downtown, neighborhood, regional, special-group, suburban, and storefront. Except for the storefronts they tend to be large, from 300 members on up into the thousands. Each owns or uses properties which may be very expansive as well as expensive. Activities are numerous and diverse: from worship and education to roller skating and Boy Scouts. Organization is extensive, but the clergy is still overworked.

Strength of the Parish in the City

The city parish has its strengths. Sheer size and financial strength may be assets. There are many people involved, and many of them are capable of rendering all sorts of service. There are physical facilities available. Many of the parishes are well organized and well led. The variety in membership generally reflects the variety in the city, and there are opportunities for service for all somewhere — although any given parish may not reflect citywide variety. Many city dwellers become members as they would join any voluntary association, yet for many others the parish provides the deeper, broader fellowship which they need and could get nowhere else. For those who participate the parish can give much that the city dweller specifically needs: a sense of the value of the individual and of the integrity of the person; close fellowship with others; a sense of significance and satisfaction in one's occupation; guidelines for moral conduct; concern for the community; purpose for leisure time; incentive to study and pursue the good, the beautiful, and the true; counsel and comfort in time of crisis and decision; opportunities for service; resources for building Christian families; security amid mobility; opportunity to combat the evils in the city; the strength to love people different from oneself; and so on. Of course there are opportunities for worship, participation in the sacraments, prayer, Christian education, mutual witnessing, Christian stewardship, and fellowship. After careful sociological study, Gerhard Lenski concludes, in *The Religious Factor,* that religious organizations in the modern world remain vigorous and influential and will probably be more so in the future. His study indicates that religion does influence daily living and secular institutions — also within modern cities. Those parishes which operate parochial schools have an even greater effect on people.

Weakness of the Parish in the City

But we must study particularly the weaknesses of parishes in cities. Size can be a liability as well as an asset. How large a flock can one man shepherd? For how large a family can one man be a father? As many as 300? This writer doubts that anyone can possibly serve adequately any more than that. Inevitably larger numbers will bring about decreasing personal relations until the shepherd cannot possibly call all his sheep by name; the father cannot guide all the members of his household. A family spirit can quickly disappear amid the numbers and impersonality of a large city parish. The same impersonality and fragmentation that go on in city life are thus reproduced within the parish, and the wholeness, the peace, is lost.

A serious weakness which flows partly from the city's impact on its people is the unwillingness on the part of many members to become personally, actively involved in the parish. They may have joined as casually as if taking membership in the "Y." They then refused to invest themselves, refuse to take personal responsibilities, and refuse to accept any position of service within the parish. The result is a shortage of willing workers and a lack of able lay leadership. Of course this has always been a problem for parishes everywhere. But it seems to be accentuated in modern city parishes.

Although much money may be available, more money is always needed. Fund raising can become too prominent in the parish program; the methods employed can offend member and outsider alike. Particularly in the central city and in changing communities, finances become a problem. The money just is not there. Yet these inner-city plants are the properties that have deteriorated the most, or are now far too large for the present membership, or are in locations where all sorts of facilities are most needed. The inner-city parish suffers along with its community as financial resources and control move to the periphery and beyond. Discouragement, pessimism, gloom, and a longing for the good old days may then engulf and immobilize laity and clergy alike.

A serious and sinful weakness exists in parishes which refuse to evangelize or welcome persons who differ from their membership in race or color or who belong to a different socioeconomic class. Are parishes that become closed community clubs fellowships of Christians in which the Spirit is being allowed to lead? Cities are made up of many kinds of people and mobility of population is one of the obvious factors in their modern life. Unwillingness and inability to adjust to this sort of change may become a problem for many parishes. Minority group members and newcomers to the cities are not being reached and served adequately by the well-established, larger groups within Christendom. If they are served at all it is by their own groups — mostly storefront missions and sects. More often than not these newcomers become disgusted with the church and are absorbed in earning a living or overwhelmed by problems of adjusting to urban life. In the course of time they are drawn away from Christian worship altogether. Yet the parish has so much to offer them, and they need it so desperately!

City mobility has many weakening effects on the parish. New members must steadily be won and assimilated, and new leaders must constantly be trained. All the problems of human relations are involved; among other necessities precise, complete records are a must. Persons who move away may remain active in a now-distant parish, or they may drift away from all Christian parishes, or they may not be fully welcomed and received into a parish near their new residence. New members within a parish may find themselves kept out of positions of leadership on the basis of a lack of seniority rather than lack of ability. Mobility, strange as it may sound, may thus play a part in the development of parish provincialism, and tradition may take full control.

The parish may fail to provide those needs already listed as especially useful for city folk, for example, guidelines for moral conduct to be applied on the job. Or it may be totally unconcerned about its community and foster civic withdrawal among its members. It may fail to enlist and train persons for service or possibly to offer them such opportunities. It may allow its own ethics to become conformed to those of the world and thus fail to offer clear guidelines in matters that disturb its members. It may confuse mere parish-program participation with Christian service; thus it further feeds the forces that secularize society.

Adoption of worldly standards of success is a common failing among city parishes (although here they may lag behind suburbia). In a world ever conscious of statistics and ever eager for success, attempting to evaluate the work of the Kingdom in this way is an ever-present temptation to everyone involved, and it has far-reaching ill effects. Comparison and competition with their weakening pressures result — between parishes of different denominations, within one denomination, or within the parish itself.

Much criticism today is directed at city parishes for their weakness in influencing their environment. Many critics contend that the parish is failing totally and that it is entirely irrelevant. Sociologist Berger has already been mentioned. A list of theologians could be given along with sociologists and scholars in other fields. One must first agree on the proper function of the parish and then proceed to precise analysis. Probably full agreement will never be reached. Yet one must acknowledge that a great deal of this criticism is just. Many individual parish members have not applied their faith fully to life; many parishes have not been the sharp edge of God's action against the world; in many ways the world seems more present in the parish than the parish in the world. There is much truth in Berger's contention that too much of American religion has simply sanctioned the social status quo and labeled this an "O. K. world." As one example, consider our failure in the past to apply our religious professions to our racial practices. Then consider our hesitancy in the present to make full applications along these lines. Clearly city parishes have not been the powerful force for good they could have been and should have been.

Many other weaknesses might be mentioned. There may be a city busyness and hastiness that produces complaints if a worship service lasts five minutes longer than usual. There may be a failure to foresee such changes as urban renewal within the community, or to plan properly to cope with change. There may be an unwillingness to experiment and allow flexibility in the program. These are examples of other, less important, weaknesses. The reader can undoubtedly add to this list.

The final weakness to be noted here: the average parish pastor! He has too many people to shepherd. He is often frustrated by a lack of willing and able lay helpers. He is often troubled by his own financial problems; he is perhaps too much involved in the fund raising of the parish; perhaps he is not sufficiently trained or experienced to oversee properly the business affairs of the parish. He himself may discriminate against persons not of his kind. He himself may foster parish provincialism — as though the parish were somehow his or as though it were the most important one in the entire Kingdom. He may be reluctant to transfer active, generous givers to other parishes — even when they obviously should go. He may have let himself become what some have called a parish director. He may have allowed himself to become regarded by spectator members as a priest who performs for them on Sundays. He may personally and privately despise city life. He may be unconcerned about community conditions or civic affairs. He is bound to have some shortcomings and blind spots, and to be subtly if not overtly pressured by the desire for worldly success. He is almost certain to feel overworked, and usually he is. He may feel overwhelmed as he considers everything he should be doing — let alone what he could be doing. He looks longingly at Acts 6 wondering what it would be like to be devoted to the preaching of the Word and to prayer. Then he remembers what he is supposed to be: Christlike Christian, loving husband, model father, reputable relative, faithful friend, good neighbor, concerned citizen; active participant in his larger church body, administrator, archivist, author, Bible student; business manager, community organizer, counselor; educational supervisor, evangelist, fund raiser, group leader; janitor, journalist, linguist, musician-if-possible, patron of the arts; pray-er, preacher, psychiatrist, public relations expert, public speaker, scholar, social worker, sociologist, teacher; visitor of the sick and shut-ins, youth expert, wedding director, and worship leader. There's no doubt about it. The pastor is one of the weaknesses within the city parish.

The Parish Listens and Responds

There is the parish — with all its strengths and weaknesses, being powerfully influenced by the city and seemingly having little effect upon its environment! There it is, mostly hidden in the midst of the modern city. Certainly it must respond; surely it must react. It hears clearly the criticisms of both those outside the church and in. It feels deeply the pains of frustration and of its failure to fulfill His plan. It returns to Him in repentance. He hears, He heals, He helps. He has never left His people; rather, He is with them always. He gives new courage, new hope, and new strength. The parish in the city resolves to respond.

How shall it respond? Let it listen carefully. Let it learn diligently. Let it consider critically. Let it grow as God the Father desires. Let it be secure in the rule of God the Son. Let it be willing to change as God the Holy Spirit leads.

"Seek the welfare of the city where I have sent you into exile, and pray to the Lord on its behalf, for in its welfare you will find your welfare" (Jer. 29:7). So the prophet Jeremiah wrote to the people of God who had been taken to Babylon. So the Spirit speaks today to the people of God in all cities.

Death and Birth of the Parish in the City

Suggestions That Seem Extreme

"Let the parish die. Let it die and remain dead. Let us be sure to bury it well." Some voices call for this response to meet the modern challenge. But in this respect these seem to be the voices of false prophets.

Through the centuries God has acted through the Word His people proclaimed. He has not only made individual persons His own but also set them into the fellowship of His people. On the day of Pentecost the Holy Spirit was given. Jesus' followers proclaimed the Word and administered the water not only that individuals might be saved but also that the body of believers might be enlarged and its activity expanded. Since the day of Pentecost the Holy Spirit has worked mightily through Word and Sacrament to bring individuals to faith in Jesus Christ, to set them into fellowship with other believers, and to nourish and further that fellowship. Christians are persons who have been born again of water and the Spirit into the family of God's people. Whether one likes it or not (and one should like it), the process of spiritual birth begins with people other than oneself and ends by placing one into a relationship with people other than oneself.

We are freely justified for Christ's sake through faith. That we may obtain this faith the ministry of teaching the Gospel and administering the sacraments was instituted. For through the Word and Sacraments, as through instruments, the Holy Spirit is given; in those who hear the Gospel He works faith where and when it pleases God. This is the way God has chosen to work, and therefore we are to give thanks and willingly serve as workers together with Him.

There are, then, local groups of God's people through whom individuals come to be born into God's family. And, being born, they are members of this family, attached to local groups of His people. A parish is a local group of God's people. It is not true, therefore, that Christians may freely choose not to become members of local parishes. People cannot become Christians at all without the prior existence of parishes. Becoming Christians, they are born into these families of believers and are then sustained as Christians within families of believers.

"Let the professional, ordained clergy die. Let them die and remain dead. Let us be sure to bury them well." So some modern voices call. Obviously here one must ask carefully for definitions, precise and practical, for both the key words. Here, depending on what is meant, the voices have a point. A ministry of Word and Sacrament is necessary. On the basis of Scripture this ministry need not be professional; it need not be ordained. But here we are thinking of absolute necessities. This does not mean that present professional, ordained clergymen should immediately resign. It does not mean that they are useless or not worth what

146

they are being paid. There certainly is a vital place for professional, ordained clergymen in modern parishes. The complexity and heightened demands of the modern world require more training than ever for those who lead God's people. Certainly Eph. 4 teaches that God chooses to set various persons with the necessary qualifications into positions of leadership among His people, and that these persons are to be regarded as precious gifts by His people. One can argue, technically, that professional, ordained clergy are not absolute necessities. But the important point is not this at all. It is rather that in addition to their present leadership city parishes can well use all sorts of ministries carried out by all sorts of people, and it is the reminder that there are many ways in which professional, ordained clergymen can serve within the Kingdom.

"Shift the concern of the parishes altogether to their communities," others suggest. Then all sorts of evidence is marshaled to prove that city parishes are unconcerned and have little if any impact on modern cities. But, as has already been noted, other bits of evidence can be assembled to prove the opposite.

It is well to bear in mind the Social Gospel movement that took place around the turn of the last century. Then, too, parishes found themselves in the midst of rapidly changing environments, overwhelmed by social problems. It is natural that at such times parishes and pastors are greatly concerned about their society. They should be. They are to be light in the world, salt for the earth, and leaven within society. They are to be active in their environment, influencing it for good, striving to do so more and more. They should be alarmed when the world seems to move farther and farther away from its Maker.

But they must also remember that the basic functions of the parish, though certainly performed within the world, are not of the world. Our citizenship is above, and only His second coming will terminate the evil and diadem the good. Parishes and pastors are to work for righteousness here and now, yet always "according to His promise we wait for new heavens and a new earth in which righteousness dwells." (2 Peter 3:13)

Death and Resurrection of the Parish

Let the parish die. But let the parish also rise. When the parish dies, it will also rise in birth. Let the parish share in Christ as fully as possible. Let it experience in some measure what He experienced. He died, and He also rose. He had to die to accomplish His purpose: that God's plan might be carried out. But He also had to rise, and for the same reason. Life out of death, or death in order that there might be birth, is one of the great themes of the Bible. Life where there was no life and no right to expect life is one of the great gifts of our gracious God.

The account of creation, the birth of Isaac to Abraham and Sarah, the birth of Jesus, the beginning of the church, the spiritual birth of each believer, dying and rising with Christ in baptism — all proclaim this Good News. "Unless a grain of wheat falls into the earth and dies, it remains alone; but if it dies, it bears much fruit" (John 12:24). To have the life of God there must first be death. So let the parish die. But let the parish also rise!

What features of the parish will rise? If the parish dies, what elements can we expect to find after its rebirth?

> — a community of God's people
> — leadership within this community
> — the use of God's Word
> — the use of Baptism and Communion
> — prayer
> — fellowship
> — discipline
> — deeds of love

148

— witness to the world

— in deeds

— in words

Bearing these in mind will help us in our analysis.

What Should Die

What in city parishes should die and stay dead? **Pride and its** partner, provincialism, must die. Pride governs too many little kingdoms and little kings or little princes and their principalities. Large size may become a goal that feeds pride, and all sorts of secular measuring sticks may be applied to supply material for boasting — silently, of course. (As though competition is what builds the kingdom of God!) Members are held onto in the face of the forces of mobility. With pride may go self-satisfaction and unconcern for the community or personal problems of members. Other Christian parishes may be unnoticed — perhaps even those in the same denomination. A parish may be called by the name of its pastor, and it is tragically more his than His. Too easily parishes become ends in themselves, instead of remaining means toward the ends of God. In *The Church and Its Ministry* David Belgum quotes a Roman Catholic priest:

> Too often pastors allow themselves to become swallowed up in the daily round; they forget that the whole is greater than any of its parts, and they act as if the church universal were confined within the periphery of their parishes. This is a fundamental mistake, with serious consequences. The universal church, as the embodiment of Christ in the world, must occupy first place in a pastor's religious purview. To this end he should not only keep himself abreast of all worldwide church movements, but in addition he should so train his people.[2]

Wherever there is pride there is bound to be a looking down on others; there will very likely be an unwillingness to accept those of different race or class. This pride must die; this provincialism must stay dead!

Materialism, too, should stay buried. Generally, one of its symptoms is "propertyolatry." Or should this be called its cause? The city parish so easily succumbs to the way of life in its environment. Its properties are certainly convenient, though one ought to underscore that property does not appear on the list of parish essentials. Its properties are also expensive. The need for more money brings about an overemphasis on fund raising. All sorts of gimmicks may be tried and all the organizations enlisted. Commercialism can crowd out religion. But even as it does, the participants — for example, the ladies busy managing the bazaar — possibly rejoice that they are for the moment serving the Lord (which may or may not be true). The image the parish thus presents to the critical outsider is one of a mercenary, mundane organization.

Social "clubbism" must die. Perhaps the parish is very easy to join. It may deliberately carry on all sorts of activities which seek to appeal to everyone in the community and draw him inside its doors on the basis of some special interest. Such an approach may not be bad, provided it is coupled with adequate education distinguishing Christian discipleship from participation in voluntary organizations. But often this is not done. In this way many parishes unwittingly foster the tendency of city dwellers to participate only impersonally, with a minimum of involvement and investment.

Traditionalism dies hard; yet we must strive to keep it under. Some find the security they need in simply perpetuating the past. "But, pastor, we've never taken the collection that way before!" "But, pastor, we've always had confirmation on Palm Sunday!" In the midst of constant change in the city, this sort of traditionalism may seem to supply needed security. The pillars of the congregation may cling to their controlling position; the forces of mobility of population and changing communities may not be able to budge them. In spite of obvious new needs there may be great difficulty in introducing experimentation or flexibility. Walter Kloetzli, in *The Church and the Urban Challenge,* is worth citing here:

> In the midst of constant and continuing change, the urban church faces continuing death and renewal. If the death or loss of congregational identity is done in His name, then the gift of new life will be provided by Him. Where the old life is protected and preserved at all costs, even to the denial of the "cup of cold water" to some of His children — then there will be death without renewal.[3]

That there may be birth after death, let us not allow traditionalism to go on living!

Activism is another plague of present-day parishes. It is part of American life simply to be active, busy, doing something. Along with materialism and social "clubbism," attending meetings can deceive many an earnest Christian. He feels he's not doing enough when he's only praying. His vocabulary has lost the word meditation. He wants organizations without inquiring as to their purpose. He's sure the youth problem is solved if only youngsters are kept off the streets. Mere parish activity for its own sake ought also die and stay dead.

Perhaps it will seem a small matter, but this writer proposes for at least partial burial the distinction sometimes made between baptized and confirmed members of a parish. To be sure, this serves some useful and legitimate purposes; for example, to designate which members are regarded eligible for Holy Communion. But too easily this distinction does someone damage. Too often stress is placed on the "baptized" rather than the "member." Too quickly we forget that baptized members are still members. How many baptized members are visited and prayed for when ill? How many are sought out individually by the shepherd when they go astray? How many are admonished properly when they fail to conform their lives to their baptismal vow? How many are dealt with according to Matt. 18 if they fail to confirm their baptism and come to Holy Communion?

How many parishes even keep accurate records regarding their children? The city world is an adult world even though its sidewalks and schools are teeming with children. Financially a child is always a liability, and besides, he cannot even vote! But our Savior died for all children too. To Him a child is as precious as an adult. If we bore this in mind, we'd make greater efforts to serve our children in every way possible. Efficient, effective Sunday schools and released-time programs would rise. Even the agency which serves the best, the Christian day school, would seem well worth its cost. But at present these responsibilities are often too easily dismissed. After all, children are only baptized members.

What Should Rise

Birth. Let parishes die and be born. Let parishes go under and come forth. Let certain elements of city parishes die and stay dead. Let other features arise. In Dennis Clark's words, concluding his *Cities in Crisis,* "to bring this Gospel to the fore in the urban life centers of modern civilization requires a recasting of traditional forms. . . . Christ, in His people, awaits a Resurrection amid the streets and towers, above the pride and willfulness of human affairs." [4]

Within the Parish

What ought to rise within the city parish? We have already listed the essential elements that we can expect to find after the death and birth of the parish. They are a Christian community and its leadership, use of Word and Sacraments and prayer, fellowship, discipline, deeds of love, and witness to the world. In general, then, the answer is these features — all cleansed and quickened and wholly devoted to God. But let's add a few comments to make certain points more specific.

The community of God's people will be fully committed. They will be disciples, not members; individually converted, not just joiners. In some way the size of the community will be dealt with. Perhaps the numbers will be deliberately limited. If not, the parish will have to be carefully organized in some way so that at least elders or deacons can preserve personal contact with all members; an adequate record system will have to be maintained.

Leadership is always crucial. The pastor is obviously the key person. The parish will nearly always follow his lead. As he himself dies to his present activity and rises to a new one he will more nearly fulfill his own calling and enable the parish to fulfill its own. For example, his refusing gratuities for administering the free sacraments of God will help the parish value the sacraments more highly and resist temptations to commercialize its Christianity. His own willingness to change, for example, to welcome a ministry to Negroes as they move into his community, will set the pattern for the parish.

In many city parishes more part- or full-time trained leadership is needed than one pastor can provide. A reborn parish will see that this ministry is supplied. Perhaps local volunteers or peace corps workers, secretary, deaconess, parish worker, youth leader, social worker, teacher, or assistant pastor are needed. Many city parishes throughout the country are finding group ministries to be a real blessing. There are some well-known examples of the use of full-time group ministries: the Chapel of the Intercession in New York; the East Harlem Protestant Parish and its counterparts in Chicago and Cleveland. There are less well-known examples where group ministries have involved particularly volunteers: Trinity Lutheran in Manhattan; Riverside Lutheran in Detroit. Of course any parish with a parochial school has an opportunity to develop a team ministry.

Full use of the Word and Sacraments, plus the response of prayer, is to be expected in parishes twice-born. Many city

153

parishes today are stressing small study groups devoted to Bible study, prayer, fellowship, in some cases also Holy Communion. By these means depersonalized, fragmented city Christians can find wholeness and personhood in the fellowship of the faith. Laymen and women are usually the leaders; private residences are frequently the meeting places. In some cases a special effort is made to first bring into such groups those who seem to be the most committed members of the parish; it is the expectation that their influence will spread. In other cases emphasis is placed on reaching couples. Many forms have been advocated by many persons; many names have been used. Whatever name or form they may have, such groups appear to be invaluable for the new life of the city parish.

Refined fellowship must also arise. Organizations have their place, provided they serve a purpose in accord with the proper functions of the parish. As such they have a vital place and may well be the best opportunity within a large parish for the individual to find the sense of community and the whole-person involvement with others which he so badly needs. Somewhere within the life of the larger parish there ought to be opportunity for every member to find fellowship in a subgroup especially suitable for him. For many such participation would provide the best means of offsetting those urban influences which bring about shriveled, depersonalized lives.

Closely linked to fellowship comes discipline. Where people care about one another they will seek and restore those who go astray. The parish that dies and rises will care. It will rebuke in love before little problems grow large. Its pastor and parishioners will find and use opportunities to speak confession and absolution to one another. It will never simply drop members' names. It will strive personally, patiently, and persistently to win them back. If the address is unknown it will retain the name on an inactive list. If the person has moved closer to a sister parish and his participation declines, the home parish will make a timely referral. It will retain responsibility until the person who has moved has been transferred or has otherwise been dealt with — even after it has requested the other pastor to be actively involved. When it must, it will declare any unrepentant person as no longer in fellowship.

New life means new resources for love. Love, not in word only but also in deed, will characterize the risen parish. Acts of kindness, first of all for those of the household of faith, will appear. A special concern will be shown in times of crisis as these arise in the life of the individuals to whom it ministers. If the parish can somehow supply it, help will be given as needed in all the problems that come to people. Help will come from within its own fellowship, or counsel will make help available from outside.

As the parish rises to new life for its Lord, there will be a growing witness to the world — first in deeds and then in words. The parish must be concerned about its community. It will strive in whatever ways possible to bring the active love of God to its world. Certainly it will welcome those arriving in its neighborhood regardless of such factors as race, color, ethnic background, socioeconomic level, or place of origin. It will be alert to special needs of newcomers to the city and as much as possible assist in their adjustment. In response to city mobility the parish will make periodic canvasses and then follow up as indicated with its witness to the Lord.

In all of this life of the new city parish there is an apparent need for flexibility. Variety makes the city. The parish must understand this and provide for it. Different people are best served by different forms of worship. Why not then provide this? Different people have different work schedules. Are not city parishes then obligated to provide varied opportunities for public worship? City people who meet but weekly need a chance to become friends. Why not provide such occasions as social hours?

Inner-city parishes often lack men to serve as leaders. Why not at times use women? Newcomers to the city have special needs. Why not try storefront missions as bridges between country and city? The gold coast, the high rise, and skid row all have their unique problems. Why not experiment and study, seek somehow to bring them to the Savior? Freedom in method, variety in approach, flexibility in program — all will be evidenced in the new life within the city parish.

New Life Between Parishes

What about new life between parishes? As a minimum there must be Christian courtesy between members of neighboring parishes which belong to different denominations. Of more immediate concern, let us think further concerning nearby parishes belonging to the same denomination. As the new life is lived within these parishes there is bound to be a closer drawing together. There will be more common concerns and joint ventures. Competition for members will cease, comparisons in successes will end, and rivalry or disregard will pass away. For the good of all there may be the sharing of the special skills of such workers as secretaries or youth leaders. Between several parishes it may be possible to employ all sorts of specialists. By working together perhaps parishes can support Christian day schools which otherwise would be impossible. Many opportunities are present for city parishes actively to promote the oneness which is part of God's plan for the entire creation. Why not capitalize, to His glory, on the nearness and interdependence of parishes?

Partner Parishes

Why not develop partner parishes? These should not be mother-daughter relationships, but partnerships. These could be not only between an inner-city parish and one in suburbia, but also between any one parish and any other, as both of them may choose.

156

It seems to this writer that here is a concept well worth both thought and effort. It would be most valuable if an inner city or declining parish would form a partnership with a solid, stable parish not too far away. Certainly there would be a possibility that the stronger parish would exercise control or dominance. This would have to be guarded against carefully and constantly, or many of the values would be lost. But I believe it could work. And I can envision many benefits flowing both ways from an arrangement in which financial and leadership resources were shared on such a basis. Of course the weaker parish would seem to be gaining more benefits — more money, more Sunday school teachers, canvassers, and so on. But there would be great benefits also for the parish on the giving end, for example, expanded opportunities for service. And are they not both seeking to spread the same Kingdom? Ought we not try any method possible that promises to extend His rule? In such functions as interparish Bible study groups there would be obvious mutual benefit.

But let us be practical. Wouldn't this simply add to the headaches of already overburdened pastors? Yes, in some ways it would. But that wouldn't matter if it would help to carry out His plan. To have a possibility of success the two pastors would obviously have to be able to work closely and well with one another. For this reason a partner-parish plan would probably have to be initiated by the pastors. A primary practical question is: could two pastors and parishes be Christian enough to carry out such a venture as forming a partner parish?

New Life Within the Church Body

Let us go beyond the parish. Let us go now beyond several parishes. But for brevity's sake let us restrict our thinking to the parishes within a given denomination within a given metropolis.

What questions may be raised or what suggestions might flow from this analysis of cities and their parishes?

The polity of the particular parish, as well as the government of the entire church body, should be reconsidered. Is a congregational polity the most effective possible? Would a federated polity or a closely-knit metropolitan polity with an even more centralized executive setup be more effective? Should some other forms be developed? Is there not freedom here according to Scripture? Has not the Spirit done this deliberately, knowing so much better than we that parishes of various times and places will need to respond to their environment in various ways? Walter Kloetzli's position, noted in *The Church and the Urban Challenge,* is well taken: "I question very seriously whether urban America can be adequately ministered to within the framework of complete congregational autonomy." And again: "Any polity may be employed by the Lutheran Church which expedites the proclamation of the Gospel and which implements the exercise of the priesthood of all believers." [5]

Could not the geographic boundaries used for administrative purposes within any given denomination be changed in accord with the age of the metropolis? Would it not make better sense? Would it not make the work of the Lord more effective? Would it not play its part in effecting the oneness He desires? Even though most cities within the state governments have not yet gained freedom from domination by less populated rural areas, ought not the risen parishes everywhere consider what is most in accord with the plan of God and govern themselves accordingly? For example, should several men in little towns 50 miles away withhold the funds and curtail the opportunities of a struggling mission parish in the heart of a central city? Or should the men in the large cities, if they have control, ignore or neglect the country parish located in a town whose name they have never heard?

Improved methods of managing money go hand in hand with improved administration. Perhaps there should be much more pooling of such resources than there is at the present time. Perhaps the vision of oneness will make us more willing to do so. But of course this adds to the burden of responsibility of those who make the decisions; those delegating authority would have to trust their decision-makers.

It would also seem that much economy could be practiced by all the parishes working together in buying and storing supplies and equipment and perhaps even in learning to share such specialists as architects and organ builders. Certainly there are problems here; there are both advantages and disadvantages to both centralization and decentralization. Let us study these problems and possible solutions thoroughly, let us put aside preconceived notions and vested interests, and as best we can discover and do what pleases our Lord.

On the metropolitan level more recognition should be given to the impact of city life on people and what this means for parishes. Increased mobility means that a greater degree of uniformity is to be desired. Those who move should be able to feel reasonably comfortable within another parish. Extremes in any area of practice, for example in liturgy, will make matters that much more difficult. Think of a person transferring from a parish where clerical collars are regarded as suspect to a parish where all are expected to cross themselves upon entering! Increased use of newspapers and mass media communications of all kinds plus the apparent extra suggestibility of city dwellers give broad hints to all the parishes to make full use of television, radio, and all the other forms of advertising and public relations.

Let all the risen parishes make fuller use of the abundant resources the Lord has made available in the form of specialists in various fields! Let them use sociologists to study the city. Let them use social workers to serve the city. Let them pool more of their resources and supply more chaplains for institutions, doctors and nurses for clinics and hospitals, counselors specially trained to serve troubled youth or quarreling couples, and agencies where employment help is offered to all. Let them relate themselves properly to the many other community agencies and resources, both public and private; let them support them, use them, not duplicate their services, but supply what may still be lacking. Let them encourage people with special interests and abilities to go out into the city and spread their Christian influence among their own particular groups.

New Life Also for the City

Of course the risen parishes are to strive to spread His rule farther and farther throughout the city. They will do this through their members as these members are nourished within the parish and are fitted for their calling. It won't happen as Christians cut themselves off from parishes and venture out on their own. The branch cannot produce fruit of itself. Risen parishes, both together and alone, will push their members out into the city harder and farther than ever before.

There will be more community concern and attempts to be of service. Words of such men as George Younger will be taken to heart. In *The Church and Urban Power Structure* he writes: "Having built its house on the sand of private preference, social aloofness, and cultural conformity, Protestantism in metropolitan areas has seen its influence steadily decline." [6] They will find some ways of speaking to the conscience of the state, at least on moral issues. Bearing in mind the Word through Jeremiah, in every way possible they will seek the welfare, the wholeness, the peace of the city. Certainly they will speak His Word of Law and strive for justice also for Negroes.

And it is to be hoped, in all this, that they will remember the value of preventing problems rather than merely treating them.

It's better to find a man a job than bring him a box of groceries —
especially when you are willing to do that only at Christmas.
Hopefully, they will in the course of time render unnecessary
a question once asked by Joseph Sittler: "Why is Lutheranism,
generally, radically Biblical in its affirmation of the Lordship of
Christ over the world, and so generally conservative toward proposals to exercise social criticism and control over the bread-
and-butter issues which have so much to do with human justice,
human intelligence in the management of life's resources, and
social arrangements for the health and happiness of the social
community?" [7]

Death and Birth Through the Word of God

How will parishes rise? What will cause them to die and then
to be born again? Rather — who? Our Savior and Lord, Jesus
Christ! He died for the sin of the world, also the sins of the
parishes. He rose from the dead and lives forevermore in and
with and for His people. He has been exalted at the right hand
of the Father. He bestows the gift of the Spirit upon the parishes.
The Holy Spirit comes to the people of the parishes today by
means of Word and Sacrament and in response to prayer. He, the
Lord and Giver of life, works new life in the parishes today. He
causes them to look carefully at the city, to listen closely, to
consider themselves in their setting. He blesses their honest,
humble study of themselves and their community. He makes
them remember the mission He has given them and confess their
failing to fulfill it. He causes them to trust the Word of pardon
and to bring forth the fruits of repentance. He works in them
an ever-increasing willingness to help carry out God's plan to
unite all things in Christ and to do so also in the midst of the
changing city.

Speaking to Nicodemus our Lord compared the Holy Spirit
with the wind. The wind is always acting, always changing, always

new. God's plan to unite all things in Christ is not yet accomplished. We want to do our full part in this process. We want to let Him work freely and fully within and through His people to accomplish His purpose in the fullness of time. For us today that means letting changes in the world be met with changes in the parishes — revolutionary changes in the urban world with comparable changes within city parishes.

As the sign of the prophet Jonah — his disappearance and emergence — was succeeded by the sign of the Savior Jesus — His burial and resurrection, so let this sign be given to the modern world — the death and birth of the parish! Toward that end let every Christian in every parish say with Paul, "I have been crucified with Christ; it is no longer I who live, but Christ who lives in me; and the life I now live in the flesh I live by faith in the Son of God, who loved me and gave Himself for me." (Gal. 2:20)

Notes

1. Walter Kloetzli, *The City Church — Death or Renewal* (Philadelphia: Muhlenberg, 1961), p. 1.

2. David Belgum, *The Church and Its Ministry* (Englewood Cliffs, N. J.: Prentice-Hall, 1963), p. 86.

3. Walter Kloetzli, *The Church and the Urban Challenge* (Philadelphia: Muhlenberg, 1961), p. 43.

4. Dennis Clark, *Cities in Crisis: The Christian Response* (New York: Sheed & Ward, 1960), p. 146.

5. Walter Kloetzli, *The Church and the Urban Challenge,* pp. 38, 39.

6. George D. Younger, *The Church and Urban Power Structure* (Philadelphia: Westminster, 1963), p. 70.

7. In Walter Kloetzli, *Challenge and Response in the City* (Rock Island, Ill.: Augustana Book Concern, 1962), p. 20.